Profit Hacking

Unlocking Revenue, Maximizing Profit, Get the Lead and Keep the Lead! - Strategies for Explosive Profit Growth in the Modern Business World

Thomas Allan

KFT
PUBLISHING

Hardback ISBN: 978-0-6457786-3-2
Paperback ISBN: 978-0-6457786-5-6
Ebook ISBN: 978-0-6457786-4-9

KFT PUBLISHING

About the Author

Introducing Thomas Allan, a dynamic author, executive coach, blogger, and influencer with a rich professional journey. His career, spanning over 30 years, has seen him excel as a psychologist, a senior sales and marketing leader, a consultant, and a business owner, always at the forefront of leadership development and revenue optimization.

Starting his career in psychology, Thomas gained an in-depth understanding of human behavior and mindset, which has become the cornerstone of his growth mindset advocacy. He then built on this foundation in his roles as a sales and marketing leader, successfully driving revenue in diverse industries through his expertise in pricing strategy, inventory management, and demand forecasting.

Thomas took his passion for growth and leadership to the next level by becoming a consultant and business owner. In these roles, he has provided expert advice and strategic direction to organizations around the globe, empowering them to achieve their potential and optimize their profitability.

Today, Thomas is the acclaimed author of "The Magnetic Mindset: Unlocking the Secrets of Influence & Persuasion" and *"Profit Hacking: Unlocking Revenue, Maximizing Profit, Get the Lead and Keep the Lead! Strategies for Explosive Profit Growth in the Modern Business World".* These transformative works draw on his extensive experience, offering readers practical, actionable steps for achieving effective leadership and explosive profit growth.

As an executive coach, he continues to guide leaders worldwide, inspiring them to adopt a growth mindset and enhance their leadership skills. He is particularly passionate about helping small business owners understand the ingredients for success in the modern business world.

Through his weekly blog, at https://magneticmindsetblog.com, Thomas continues to influence a growing audience with insights into mindset development, leadership, and profit optimization.

Thomas Allan is truly a multifaceted professional, combining his wide-ranging experience and knowledge to inspire and empower individuals and organizations. His influence extends beyond his writings, reaching those he coaches and consults to succeed personally and professionally, making a significant impact in today's fast-paced business landscape.

Also By Thomas Allan

You can subscribe to my blog for more updates and articles:
https://magneticmindsetblog.com/

a
https://magnet-mind.com/book

in
https://magnet-mind.com/linkedin

Reviews

Thomas Allan's Other Books

Kindle Customer *5.0 out of 5 stars* **"Eye-opening game changer!"**

Verified Purchase The book offers direction on how you can retrain your mindset, break out of the status quo, and expand your potential. I found the advice and practical strategies you can use to help improve and gain influence in your leadership role to be very effective and relatable. There are so many areas of advice such as public speaking and employee engagement. It will be a welcome reference book.

***

Amazon Customer *5.0 out of 5 stars* **"A must read"**

Verified Purchase The Magnetic Mindset is a captivating and thought-provoking book that offers valuable insight on the power of influence and persuasion. It provides an understanding human psychology and behavior. I would recommend The Magnetic Mindset to anyone looking to improve their leadership abilities. The book is engaging and informative.

Contents

Introduction

What L2RM Is

What is Lead to Revenue Management (L2RM), and why should you care?

What it is: L2RM is converting leads into paying customers and optimizing the process to maximize revenue.

Why you should care: You want your business to be profitable, and you want to impact your firm's success.

What You May Think L2RM Is

Sure, you're thinking, *I get it*; *L2RM is getting and keeping customers while making the most of the money earned from the deals.*

Now, you're reconsidering if you've totally grasped the concept of L2RM. You're pausing because you have several questions that remain unanswered.

That sounds great, but what actions do I take in order to attract and retain customers, and what are some proven processes for making the most of the revenue you're musing?

Let's take a poetry break that will give us an alternate view of L2RM.

An Alternate Perspective on L2RM

"Poetry! What? Didn't I get this book from the Business section?" you're asking.

Trust the process and keep reading...

In Linda Miller's poem, *The Dash*, she noted that tombstones commemorate a life by stating a birth date and a death date, separated by a dash. The dash represents all the thoughts and actions between the two dates. Miller emphasized the importance of everything enacted and experienced between the start and the end.

Across multiple industries and business sectors, the concept of L2RM is the dash between the date a sales opportunity is discovered and the date the contract is extended for another term.

In order to succeed, a business must make "the dash" count. You are mission-critical to making "the dash" count!

Your Role in L2RM

Are you asking, "*Who, me? I'm not mission-critical!*" You might be muttering to yourself one of the phrases below in support of the idea that your role is not mission-critical to L2RM.

"I make dozens of cold calls to potential customers. I'm not really in a strategic role."

"I'm a pricing analyst. I focus on base cost, markup, and quantity management. I have zero interaction with sales leads or the customer life cycle."

"I live and breathe in terms of inventory. What's in stock, where is it, and how soon can it be available for shipment; that's all I care about. That's why my title is 'Inventory Manager.'"

"I am on the hook for quality control checks and am solely responsible for ensuring the four logistics systems talk to each other. As an operations manager, I already wear too many hats, and I don't have time for anything else!"

"Numbers are my game, and data miner is my name." (We are willing to bet no one actually says that, at least not out loud or before Happy Hour starts.)

"My team takes care of tracking our customers, from onboarding them to retaining them. I only get involved when it comes to strategy."

Have you uttered any of those comments or ones similar to them? If you have, we're here to tell you that you are a mission-critical part of L2RM within your business. In the upcoming chapters, we'll explain why those who are in the roles above have a direct impact on L2RM.

L2RM as The Dash

Remember our assertion that "The concept of L2RM is the dash between the date a sales opportunity is discovered and the date the contract is extended for another term." We're making a commitment to guide you through the ever-changing and ever-challenging business landscape with L2RM as your GPS.

Our book is a trusty toolbox and not a basket of buzzwords. As such, you'll be able to start, enhance, or fine-tune your L2RM skill set through these actionable concepts.

- Realize the power of pre-sales processes, such as research and targeting.

- Generate and nurture sales leads.

- Concentrate on conversion and the critical period that follows.

- Lean into lead management.

- Tap into today's technologies.

- Learn the linchpins of revenue management: pricing strategy, inventory management, and demand forecasting.

- Make the most of measuring and metrics.

- Own optimization.

- Expand your analytical prowess to make the most of your data through real-time pricing, dynamic pricing, data mining, and predictive analytics.

The list above just gets us started on our journey. However, the next time you're playing Cards Against Humanity (Cards Against Humanity. 2010. Cards Against Humanity LLC: Chicago), rest assured you'll have an answer if the card states, "Name three L2RM skills."

Your Questions About L2RM

We've identified several actions you'll be able to take (with confidence) as you read *Lead to Revenue Management*. We're already guessing some of the questions you might have.

"How do the concepts of revenue management (e.g., pricing strategy, inventory management, etc.) affect the various parts of a business organization?"

"Informed decisions pertaining to setting prices, forecasting demand, and managing inventory will ensure the health of my company. How can I use data and analytical tools to make these types of informed decisions?"

"Technology and techniques involving sophisticated methods such as predictive analytics and dynamic pricing sound really great, but how do I actually use them?"

"How can I take the strategies we formulated and turn them into practices that can be implemented?"

"When I am in the C-suite, the first question I'll get is, 'How do you know the revenue management efforts are working?' How do I measure and then show quantitative proof the efforts are in effect?"

"What are the best companies doing when it comes to revenue management? Even if they're in a different industry, surely some of the practices are replicable."

"What's trending in revenue management, and how do I keep up?" (This is a very reasonable question. "Trending" existed long before TikTok did.)

"We've had more than one consulting team on site, tasked with examining our revenue management procedures. They had some innovative ideas but also borrowed our watch to tell us the time. Beyond the basics, what else can I do to drive more revenue and profit?"

Our Answers About L2RM

Assuming one or more of the questions matched yours, are we mind readers? No.

Do we know (word-for-word) what your business needs in terms of revenue management strategies? No.

Do we see quick fixes and plug-and-play technology as solutions? No.

Why read another book when you're praying for an extra hour in the day (which you would spend reading emails)? Why read another business book?

1. With 30 years spent across multiple industries and inside a variety of companies, we may not read minds, but we have met some of the best and brightest minds. We've woven their best practices with our vast experiences to create your go-to book for

all things related to revenue management.

2. We assume your business needs are nuanced, and while we wouldn't slap a simple strategy on the table, we've sat at countless tables across from many clients. We've seen what works and what wilts. We're going to give you what we have learned from those lessons but condensed from years to however fast a reader you are.

3. As standalone solutions, quick fixes frequently fail, and technology teeters. We can put quick fixes to work while working out a fuller fix. We know that the "technology-as-king" approach is about as useful as an emperor with no clothes. Thus, we can winnow the welter of tech tools to find the ones that you can put to work for you. A note on that: We will examine the tech tools and convey their unique attributes in a way that will make sense, even if you don't love reading software manuals.

What Keeps You Up At Night

So, what is it that keeps you up at night?

We aren't starting a round of Cards Against Humanity (Cards Against Humanity. 2010. Cards Against Humanity LLC: Chicago), amusing as it may be to have a business version. Oh, wait, we do. It's called *The Office*.

Seriously, though, we have some idea of what keeps you up at night. Said in a less stalker-like way, we think we're attuned to your worries.

Attention, Revenue, and Inventory Managers

If you're a revenue manager, you're pondering price-setting strategies to help establish price points that are neither too high nor too low. As an inventory manager, you strive to forecast demand accurately. You don't want an excess supply, which will wreak havoc when it comes to inventory management.

Here is a special note for those of you who are in the role of "inventory management" in the professional services sector. You, too, feel the stress of forecasting, though your "inventory" are people, and the demand is for their expertise. Perhaps you're not titled as an "inventory manager" when you work for a law firm and are partially responsible for assigning lawyers and paralegals to cases. Yet, you know the criticality of having the right number and correct mix of people assigned to a case.

Perhaps, in these roles, you have a deeper appreciation for revenue management concepts as they recur frequently in your day-to-day interactions. However, even the most seasoned revenue manager may be surprised at the interdependence that exists among the functions of pricing, inventory tracking, and demand projection. We'll be sure to get into the connections within those interdependencies, too.

Calling All Marketing and Sales Managers

As a marketing manager, you are responsible for driving revenue by positioning the product (or service) and spreading the word. Marketing managers know the value of product placement and can launch a campaign in their sleep.

As a sales manager, you affect revenue by bringing the customers in. Sales managers delve into demos and score with social media.

By understanding the importance of revenue management practices, sales, and marketing professionals can have an even bigger impact by integrating the practices into their business activities.

Psss… Pricing Analysts

As a pricing analyst, you're tracking industry standards, studying pricing models, and using your magnificent math skills to analyze the price points for the products or services offered by your business. An understanding of revenue management can help you see how your numbers fit into the overall financial health of the firm.

Over Here, Operations Managers

"I want our firm to be less efficient," said no CEO, ever. The first person to whom they look to ensure the business is running at maximum efficiency is you, operations manager! You probably spend much of your day organizing, planning, and strategizing in order to have productivity gains and waste reductions.

Oversimplifying to make a point, think of a business that makes $1,000,000 in profit in one year. The business nets $700,000 after taxes. Through productivity gains and waste reduction, the business avoids spending $150,000, which adds back to the $700,000. The $150,000 isn't generated by profit gains but has a similar effect. The processes and systems you implemented to achieve the productivity gains and waste reduction amplify the effect of revenue.

Search No More, Entrepreneur

When you have created, devised, and launched your own business, you feel every revenue fluctuation. A solid background in revenue management can help you make the most of what you make while you grow.

Hey, Study Buddy

Maybe you're in school and haven't entered the workforce yet. Perhaps you've taken a break from what you've done for 20 years to start fresh in a new industry. Okay, you don't have revenue to worry about yet. However, you can benefit from learning the ways revenue management techniques can guide you as you get started on your first job or in a new job.

The Lead to Revenue Management Prequel

We're going to take a lead (we chose that term on purpose) from *The Phantom Menace* for a moment. It was filmed in 1999, which is 22 years after *Star Wars* debuted on the big screen. However, the events that unfolded in *The Phantom Menace* happened chronologically before the events depicted in *Star Wars*.

While a sales lead must be generated before it can be managed, we're going to examine lead management before we examine lead generation. We'll save the deep dive into lead generation for the next chapter.

Why would we do that, other than our need to emulate George Lucas?

Establishing a foundation of broad lead management knowledge is a prerequisite to seeing how it is interwoven with revenue management. Having an overview of how the two concepts intermingle—before going into a detail-rich book—will allow you to get the most from the rest of the book.

The Relevance of Lead Management Today

Perhaps you've heard the phrases, "It's like trying to nail gelatin to a wall" or "I'm attempting to hit a moving target." Both of the phrases are accurate descriptions of what it is like for a business to stay relevant and competitive in today's marketplace.

We'll ask a rhetorical question. "What makes today's marketplace so challenging?" Where do we begin (another rhetorical question)?

1. Information is disseminated at warp speed.

2. Technological innovations happen in a blink of an eye, as one tool is built upon another.

3. Independent publishing has allowed great business minds to

have access to the spotlight, which previously was reserved for similarly great business minds (with the largesse of capital, time, and connections).

With challenges like these, it's more critical than ever before to drive sales and increase revenue…as quickly as possible! Both of those actions begin with lead management, which is a cornerstone of the L2RM process.

The Major Components of Lead Management

Defining Lead Management

Lead management is finding people or organizations who may be potential customers (identifying a lead), determining how your business can address their needs (qualifying a lead), and then selling your product or service offering to them in order to meet their needs (converting a lead).

Identifying Potential Leads

In order to identify a potential lead, a business needs to learn about an individual's or individuals' unmet needs. There are various querying methods a business can use to find out what its potential market is missing. Querying methods include online forms, web analytics, and social media monitoring.

Online Forums

Businesses can create online forms and make them available on their website. Potential customers complete the forms and submit them electronically. The data put into the forms flows to an electronic repository maintained by the business. Analysts evaluate the data. The analysts present the data in a variety of ways in order to demonstrate trends, interest, strength of interest, etc. Once the data is condensed and organized so that it tells a story, the analysts present it to various management teams. The managers will make strategic decisions based on what they have learned.

Web Analytics

Every day, internet surfers visit websites. Through a tool known as web analytics, user behavior is analyzed. The user behavior may be the number of clicks on a link, number of rage clicks, or when most of the users view the website. Web analytics can convey how people are visiting and accessing a website. Similar to online forms, web analytics provide information about people who are visiting the business's website. Web analytics identify and track actions performed by those visiting a website, like clicking links or downloading a program.

Social Media Monitoring

Social media monitoring tells a business about the reactions to their products or services by what is shared among users through online forums, discussion groups, and apps. Social media monitoring uses publicly available information to provide insights about the website visitors.

Search engines examine websites and collect data from them, such as keywords or other signals. Based on what the search engine has culled from a website, it decides where to place the website when a specific word or words are queried. Paid search results and organic search results. Every click costs the advertiser a paid search result. Organic search results come up based on SERPs.

Qualifying Leads

Once a business has gathered the data (the types of which are listed above), they determine if the potential customer's needs match what they can provide. In a business-to-business situation, one business selling to another, determinations can be made by reviewing the potential customer's budget, project timeline, and potential hurdles.

Imagine this situation: an international steel manufacturer, Steel the Best, is the business that wants to sell its steel to a construction company, Elaine & Sons, Inc. Elaine & Sons, Inc. is erecting a 101-story hotel in Dubai. Steel the Best needs to know how much steel is required, the specifications and types of steel, as well as Elaine & Sons, Inc.'s budget and project plan. Elaine & Sons, Inc. requires high-strength low-alloy steel beams, however, Steel the Best has limited quantities of it. In this case, Steel the Best has to decide if Elaine & Sons, Inc. is a qualified lead.

In a business-to-consumer situation, in which a business is selling to an individual, similar determinations are made. The decisions are smaller in scale but can affect many individuals' buying choices.

Canadian retailer, Lululemon, is known for its high-quality (and expensive) exercise clothing. Lululemon encourages online reviews. They often address individual negative reviews with helpful suggestions or, in some situations, offer to refund the customer's money. The feedback teaches Lululemon about their customer base. Their retail stores offer free yoga classes and water-filled bowls for the shoppers' pets. Do you think they'd offer free bags of potato chips? Notwithstanding their more colorful shorts, do you anticipate that Lululemon will start a line of fluorescent-hued hunting apparel? Probably not. They know their customer base. They create new lines of clothing and a welcoming atmosphere in their stores aimed at the comfort and interests of their customers.

Nurturing Leads

After a lead is qualified, the business focuses on building rapport and continuing to learn about the potential customer. These actions increase the chance the potential customer will convert to becoming a customer.

Rapport is built through selective communication with the potential customer, as well as being quick to provide any additional information.

A business wants the potential customer to know they (the business) are educating themselves on their (potential customer) needs.

During the phase of nurturing a lead, a business may focus on content marketing. Content marketing shows a potential customer that the business understands them and grasps their pain points.

Consider the following situation: a business consulting firm wants to convert a major U.S. automaker who doesn't offer an electric or hybrid vehicle. The business consulting firm shares with the automaker some publicly available material that addresses the positive qualities of automobiles reliant on fossil fuels.

Tracking and Monitoring Leads

The numbers of leads identified, qualified, and nurtured are important. That said, often, there is a lot of time between lead nurturing and the point when the potential customer "signs on the dotted line" (i.e., legally agrees to accept product or services at an agreed price with specified terms).

What happens after the lead nurturing phase? How does a business know the effects of lead nurturing? If the Chief Revenue Officer (CRO) asks a sales analyst for the status of March's lead identifications, the sales analyst should have a weightier response than "They're looking good." This is where lead tracking and monitoring become relevant.

The actions of lead tracking and monitoring allow a business to see how potential customers are moving through the sales process. Technology can be immensely useful for this phase of lead management. In its basic form, a lead management system records each qualified lead and keeps track of what happens to it. The system relies on the employees involved to log the contact information for the lead, as well as the events related to the lead (e.g., "Had first follow-up teleconference with ABC Company. The ABC Company project manager will provide a go or no go decisions in ten days.")

Maximizing the Value From Tracking and Monitoring Leads

To get the maximum benefit from a lead management system, the business's employees must be diligent about entering data into it, and the leaders need to be aware of the stories the data tells. The data will tell a story for each lead. The leads that didn't become customer conversions will have a log of information associated with them. This helps with the identification of weak areas in the process by which the business tries to convert potential customers into customers.

We know that it is Utopian and unreasonable to think that employees can make time to create a detailed entry regarding each qualified lead or that leaders can reasonably review the status of the qualified leads in order to determine where the procedural weak links are. However, if particular leads are deemed high-value (e.g., a very large-dollar opportunity or a strategic opportunity), a lead management system can be customized to flag them in a way that makes them easily trackable.

Additionally, a lead management system acts as a continual feed of up-to-date information on potential customers and customers. A lead management system can tell you what your customers want, how frequently the sales representatives are following up with prospects, and the events that preceded upticks in inbound customer communication. Ultimately, you can tailor your products or services to convert or retain. It's an example of working smarter, not harder. Pouring hours into researching how to improve the design of charging stations for your customer, an electric automobile maker, is a waste of time if the electric automobile maker's charging modules consistently earn high ratings from Consumer Reports.

Finally, a lead management system offers a way for a business to stay organized and efficient in terms of the customer data it captures.

The End of the Prequel

With a broad overview of lead management set in place, we're going to end the prequel. Now, we're going to work chronologically. It's easiest to see the full picture if we start with a numbered list of the steps, in order, from lead generation to revenue management.

From Lead Generation to Revenue Management, Step-by-Step

Chronologically, these are the steps that will be covered in depth:

1. Lead generating

2. Lead nurturing

3. Lead converting

4. Lead management

5. Revenue management

6. Results measurement

In a very simple example, we'll tie specific actions to the aforementioned steps. In future chapters, when we do a deep dive into each of the steps, we will focus on complex examples.

An In Real Life (IRL) Example of L2RM

For now, let's stop at the Harford Hardware Store (HHS). We'll meet an HHS employee, Megan, and a shopper, Sheldon.

Lead Generation in Action

HHS kicks off a lead generation when they post on their social media page, advertising a two-for-one hammer sale. At this time of year, in May, several shoppers go to HHS to buy flats of spring flowers, garden tools, and Mother's Day gifts.

Lead Nurturing in Action

They aren't interested in buying a hammer, let alone two of them. The HHS employees still let them know about the deal, which is lead nurturing.

One of the shoppers who is searching for spring flowers is named Sheldon. Sheldon stops to think about the window box in which he will plant the spring flowers. The HHS employee, Megan, asks him if he has a question. Sheldon tells her the window box is falling apart.

Continuing the effort of nurturing a lead, Megan informs him there are window box kits for sale in aisle seven. She adds that they don't come with a hammer. She also points out that the window box cannot be built without a hammer.

Lead Conversion in Action

Sheldon remembers he lost his hammer while building houses with his church youth group last summer. He shares that story with Megan. Megan tells him about the hammer sale. Sheldon agrees to buy a hammer but wonders aloud what he will do with two hammers. Megan points out that Mother's Day and Father's Day are coming up soon. If either of his parents are interested in building, he has scored a free gift. Megan has converted a lead successfully.

Lead Management in Action

Next, Megan puts her lead management skills to work in three ways. First, she reminds Sheldon about the window box kit. Second, she asks him if he needs assistance getting to his vehicle. Third, she informs him that if he wants some help (carrying a flat of spring flowers and a bag of two hammers is awkward), she will have someone from the packing department help him. Sheldon declines the help.

Megan leads Sheldon to the checkout counter. She tells him about the frequent shopper card, which is free to any shopper. For every $25 purchase, HHS adds a sticker to the card. After ten stickers, the shopper receives a 30% discount on their next purchase. Megan offers the card. Sheldon accepts the card.

Megan knows that all HHS employees are expected to help with revenue management. Contributing to the effort, Megan turns to her employer-issued tablet. She taps the customer relationship management (CRM) application icon and enters Sheldon's contact details. Within a CRM entry field, she electronically checks a box to indicate Sheldon has accepted the frequent shopper card.

Analytics in Action

HHS Corporate is tracking the acceptance of frequent shopper cards. The HHS revenue manager and HHS inventory specialists are studying the impact of the frequent shopper cards. Through the data gathered in their CRM application, HHS is tracking the purchases made by the frequent shopper card holders. Additionally, they are tracking how long it takes each cardholder to make ten purchases of $25 or more and earn a 30% discount. Finally, they are tracking what the customers choose to purchase with the 30% discount and whether they make other purchases at the same time. HHS Corporate wants to know if the frequent shopper card program is driving profitability.

Falsehoods and Truths About L2RM

We are going to wrap up the Introduction by sharing some fiction and a few falsehoods about L2RM. Who doesn't love a bit of fake news to enliven a day?

Example One

Falsehood One: Revenue management is a singular business function. It means managing a business's money with a primary focus on prices.

Truth One: Revenue management isn't a standalone concept, hence the "L2" part of L2RM. Lead to revenue management is a flow of processes.

Revenue management is about prices, yes, but not only about prices. Evaluating data from the sales life cycle, inventory, and distribution is what revenue management entails.

In addition to prices, the customer experience also matters. Seeing and understanding customer experiences requires research and communication. Don't forget about the "silent costs" (e.g., taxes and fees) the business has to bear, those must be tallied as well.

Finally, keep in mind the logistical practicalities, such as the availability and accessibility of the product or service. One may be in the business of manufacturing soda, but the thirsty masses won't wait outside your factory doors for a sip of carbonated deliciousness. A soda manufacturer needs to make the product available and accessible to the people. That translates into transportation, fuel costs, drivers, pallets, and the list goes on. As none of those resources are free or instantly claimable, time and money are needed.

It's easy to forget that managing revenue is more than the price of the product or service.

Example Two

Falsehood Two: Revenue management is only relevant to selling stuff, such as hotel rooms or plastic injection parts. "Business" just means selling products at prices that allow one to make a profit after paying for the base costs.

Truth Two: Business has blown beyond selling stuff. Businesses make money by providing products as well as services. Businesses sell everything from storage space to data, from fictional money (think of the currencies of online games like Fortnite and Roblox) to periods of time for electric scooter use. (We're serious; many major cities offer scooter rentals for a predetermined period of time. Rental locations, maps, and fee payment options are accessible through an app.)

Also, one has to consider the shifts occurring in our society. There is a shift from buying stuff to paying for information and experiences. There is a shift toward real interest in corporate responsibility, environmental sustainability, and ethical sourcing; these concerns lived in the background only a few decades ago. Important as they are, those practices take time to establish. That means that a business must be ever diligent in managing its revenue!

Example Three

Falsehood Three: Revenue managers need to look only at supply and demand levels in order to drive profits.

Truth Three: Supply and demand levels matter. However, revenue managers must take into account a vast number of factors. They consider seasonality, competitor pricing, and even weather.

Sporting goods stores don't count on selling the largest volume of paddleboards in July; similarly, they wouldn't spend thousands of dollars on a marketing campaign for new-to-market jet skis in December. You've seen this at work in your daily life. Think of the advertisements for temporary retail employees during the holiday season that spans November and December.

Do you think competitor pricing doesn't matter? Take a look backward, approximately 20–23 years ago, and consider the brokerage market. Electronic brokers like e*trade stormed the staid financial services scene, offering low-price brokerage services. Discount trades plummeted from $30 per trade to $8 per trade (Rao, Bergen, Davis, 2000).

Try telling the agribusiness (e.g., commercial and non-commercial farming outfits, fisheries, etc.) industry that the weather doesn't matter. Temperature spikes, unanticipated rainfall, and unseasonable cold spells can trounce razor-thin profit margins.

<u>A Fun Fictional Example</u>

Nothing emphasizes the importance of a multitude of factors affecting a business decision the way HBO's *Silicon Valley* does. There's a perfect scene in the third episode of the first season of the television show. We guarantee you will never look at Burger King food the same way ever again, at least not without thinking of cicadas (stay with us, we're going somewhere with this!).

Character Peter Gregory is a venture capitalist who is quite brilliant and extremely quirky. Gregory set up a demonstration involving Burger King menu items. In his demonstration, he communicated the importance of interconnectivity among apparently unrelated factors.

"Burger King sandwiches have sesame seeds. Brazil and Myanmar, which supply much of the world's sesame seeds, are about to face the worst cicada infestation in two centuries. But Indonesia also grows sesame seeds but has no cicada population. So, Gregory buys up a bunch of Indonesian sesame seed futures and gives the founders the loan they need out of the project profits of this purchase" (Borghese, Turbovsky, 2014. paragraph 3).

Example Four

Falsehood Four: Revenue management is a static process, with data that can be revisited quarterly.

Truth Four: Fueled by the factors we mentioned earlier (e.g., technology, the speed of information dissemination, etc.), revenue management has to be dynamic in nature and evaluated frequently. Otherwise, by the time a business responds, it may be too late.

Example Five

Falsehood Five: By buying software and subscribing to real-time data feeds, a business can glean all the quantitative information it needs. Employees need only to read the outputs from the software and data feeds.

Truth Five: Technology (and its outputs) is only as helpful as the people who are studying it and working with it. Complex algorithms and machine learning are the workhorses beneath the slick software. A business needs to have a working understanding of what these tools do in order to use them effectively. How can you tell a story if you don't understand the plot?

A Last Word

We admit, for an introduction, this was a long one. We think you'll agree that L2RM is a subject that is broad, deep, and nuanced to the point that a detailed overview is useful.

You have a succinct understanding of what L2RM is and the cross-section business professionals (e.g., revenue managers in addition to inventory managers, etc.) involved with L2RM components.

We identified the pain points that may keep you up at night. Did we name any of yours?

We mimicked George Lucas by skipping the first step of L2RM (it will be revisited later in the book, we promise.) We focused on lead management, briefly dissecting the actions (e.g., identifying leads, qualifying leads, nurturing leads) that comprise it.

Fictional characters Megan and Sheldon walked us through a very simple rendering of the complete L2RM process. Next time you're stuck in a long line at your local home improvement store, study the interactions between the employees and customers. You might see real-life Megan and Sheldon.

Finally, we debunked and dismissed five misconceptions about revenue management. We'll consider it a bonus if we made you laugh a little at the sesame seeds example, brilliantly portrayed in *Silicon Valley*.

Chapter One

Understanding Lead Generation

What Lead Generation Is

What is lead generation, and why should you care?

What it is: Lead generation is a set of processes for finding and obtaining potential customers for a business.

Why you should care: Without attracting interested parties to what your business is selling, your business will have no sales. A business with no sales has a 100% chance of failing.

What You May Think Lead Generation Is

When you hear the words "lead generation," do you picture a person sitting at a desk with a phone crunched between their shoulder and ear? Do you assume they've been contacting companies by calling the main number, pressing "0" for the operator, and then asking to speak with anyone in the business development department? Do you think they have a pre-printed script in front of them, with something like the following typed on it: "Good morning/afternoon! I am from Company RST and have a great offer on windows I'd like to tell you about."

That is only one method of lead generation known as "cold-calling." It's the act of making unsolicited contact in person or by telephone in order to sell a product or service.

Lead generation is broader and deeper than one way of doing it (i.e., cold-calling). Let's get beyond "It's a set of processes for attracting customers."

An In-Depth Look at Lead Generation

While every business dreams of having a product or service that draws in potential customers organically (interested parties come to your business on their own), it's much more likely that a business needs to be proactive in drawing the potential customers to itself.

We can't overstate the importance of lead generation. Nothing in the sales cycle nor the revenue management process would exist without lead generation. From your business's vantage point, lead generation is where it all begins.

Let's skip ahead a bit and be optimistic. Assume your business has attracted potential customers. It's been established that your business has what the potential customers want. The potential customers become paying customers; the conversion is complete! Is your lead generation work completed?

No.

Wait, you're thinking, my business drew in strangers and offered them a product or service. My business cultivated their interest, at which point they became potential customers. Then, they signed the sales agreement, and the deal was inked! The payments are on the way! The sale is a success story.

Yes, that is a success story…for one sale. Is the one customer going to be your sole source of revenue? Is the one product or service for which they signed a contract going to be enough to allow a profit margin?

No. Most businesses require more than one customer. Also, most businesses want to continue to sell the same product or service to an existing customer, but also introduce them to other products and services the business offers. Lead generation needs to be an ongoing first step.

There's the lead generation that bears fruit when the potential customer becomes a qualified lead. However, there exists the generation of leads for expanded or new sales.

An Example of Lead Generation Leading to Additional Lead Generation

Your business offers the service of filing corporate tax returns. Your customers are in the food services sector; among them are beverage manufacturers, bakers, and meat processing plants.

A meat processing plant, Herd Today Gone Tomorrow, is a current customer. They have relied on your tax service for five years. Is there an opportunity for lead generation with Herd Today Gone Tomorrow?

At first glance, it may seem like there are no opportunities. Taxes are due once per year. There isn't a need to engage a tax preparer more than once per year.

What are some other activities that go along with tax filing (no, falling asleep does not count)? Can you think of any?

With Herd Today Gone Tomorrow, you know your employees that go to their head office complain a lot. Once onsite, they always end up waiting an extra day or two while Herd Today Gone Tomorrow locates and gathers their tax forms, receipts, and other official documents.

Wouldn't Herd Today Gone Tomorrow benefit from an additional service that kicks in prior to tax filing? Your business could offer a pre-tax preparation service of helping to locate and gather the materials you'll need.

As your employees are already in the door (literally) at Herd Today Gone Tomorrow, it's a great conversation starter. As a couple of beleaguered Herd Today Gone Tomorrow employees pull open filing cabinets and tear through boxes of documents, one of your employees might mention their ability to pop in a day or two earlier to assist in document gathering.

Then, one Herd Today Gone Tomorrow employee sighs loudly because they've discovered they are out of envelopes and the ink cartridge is so empty the print on the documents looks like invisible ink. Your employee comments that they have supplies on hand, which they can bring, too.

A new lead is generated with an existing customer!

Methods of Lead Generation

There are as many methods of lead generation as there are fish in the sea. Okay, that is an exaggeration, but we aren't kidding when we state that lead generation can take all manner of forms.

On any one day, you have been exposed to many lead generation methods.

A Day in Your Life Experiencing Lead Generation

Lead Generation Method: Content Marketing

After you open your eyes, what is the first thing you do in the morning? Do you pick up your phone or tablet to check the news headlines? As you scroll through the paragraphs of a lead story, you see an image of a person fishing with nothing around them but a lake and some mountains. The image is captioned with, "Is it time for your next getaway? Your first stay with Va-Voom Vacays is 15% off when you book now!"

That is your first contact with a method of lead generation. It's called content marketing. Content marketing is the process of creating and distributing critical content with the mission of bringing in and engaging leads. Content marketing relies on images, videos, blogs, and videos.

Lead Generation Through Social Media

After you've finished catching up with current events, you open your social media applications. In between your best friend from high school's fifteenth post about his son's wedding and your trainer's weekly post about clean eating, you see a post from your colleague at work.

Your colleague's post trumpets: "J.B. Coworker's ideal place to live is: Flathead Lake, Montana. Click to take the quiz, sponsored by Real Estate Company ABC!"

As you'd rather take a two-second quiz than see another post about a day spent sampling cakes or a reminder that breakfast pastries are like glue for your arteries, you click on the quiz. After you complete the quiz and discover you should pick up and move to Provo, Utah, an ad pops up. The ad is for Real Estate Company ABC, where an agent with a dazzling smile urges you to take advantage of record-low interest rates.

That's your second contact with a method of lead generation. It's lead generation through social media. Social media is any platform in which users engage with each other through exchanging thoughts, ideas, pictures, videos, and stories.

Lead Generation Method: Referrals

You head out and catch the bus into the city. Two stops after yours, your colleague, J.B., boards. Plopping next to you in the vacant seat, J.B. mumbles a "hello," and continues to read through his automobile magazine. You ask if J.B. is looking into a new car. J.B. rolls his eyes as he tells you about his pickup truck having a rusting frame, which was uncovered during the annual inspection. Recalling your positive experience buying your pre-owned SUV, you tell him about the dealer that sold it to you. You mention that the SUV was as its paperwork claimed, and you negotiated successfully for $1,000 off the price.

You just did a little bit of work for the dealership by giving a referral to J.B.! A referral is another method of lead generation. Referrals are a type of lead generation that has been around for hundreds of years.

"I am tired of these stupid dinosaurs trampling villages and people. I wonder if dinosaurs are scared of images that look like them. Perhaps I can hire an artist to draw a dinosaur in the sand outside my village. That said, artists are scarce these days since they're all drawing on cave walls. I wonder who else might be willing to make a dinosaur face in the sand?"

"My bricks need to be cleaned before they can become part of these pyramids. I don't have time to clean them, and also, messing with their surfaces kicks up a ton of dust. My tunic gets dirty enough. It's a shame that my existing teams are busy making bricks, drying them, and assembling them into temples. Where should I go to get brick cleaners?"

"I need a seaworthy vessel for my trip to the fabled New World. To whom should I go for a cutting-edge design and a reasonable price?"

"Who makes the best bread in the village? Do they make a whole-grain loaf?"

"Where should I go to have my horse re-shoed? The new horse I just purchased is extremely unpleasant, and neither my husband nor I can get shoes put on the hooves without risking head trauma."

"My wife is attending a coronation and needs an opulent hat. Who is the best milliner in the city who also has access to fresh flowers?"

Going back to the present… your third contact with lead generation methods originated with you.

Lead Generation Method: Search Engine Optimization (SEO)

As you hurry off the bus in front of your office building, you literally run into Delaney. Delaney reminds you of the meeting you have with her at 10:00 a.m.

"For what? I forgot!" you exclaim, running through the blocks on your electronic calendar.

"You agreed to give me content for my SEO article I'm doing to promote our place at the upcoming trade show," Delaney sighs.

"SEO?" you ask.

"Search engine optimization," Delaney explains. "Remember, our firm is introducing our Supreme Super Solar Panels at the tradeshow. We're working with PR to get an attention-grabbing headline out there before the trade show starts next Wednesday."

"Got it, I think," you say, somewhat confused.

Delaney notices that you are visibly flummoxed.

"SEO is that way of writing content, so search engines pick up on it," says Delaney.

"Ideally, the search engines list our article high in the search results," Delaney goes on to explain.

"High?" you ask.

"Yes, so if you're searching for a story about pandas and penguins playing together at the zoo, the articles written about the subject use the right keywords in order to be placed at or near the top of the list of results," Delaney says.

"Right! We had a presentation on that," you reply.

"Great. So, now that we covered that, I will see you in a couple of hours. I expect some great content ideas!" Delany shouts as you board the elevator.

There you have your fourth touch point with a lead generation method, SEO.

Lead Generation Method: Trade Shows and Events

After your meeting with Delaney concludes, you remember you need to book your travel and hotel for the energy conservation event, Zappzz, which takes place starting next Wednesday.

A slight feeling of dread washes over you. You remember your role in pushing the marketing budget to accommodate the tiny solar panel keychains to be handed out at Zappzz.

"This better prove to be more than a cute toy that ends up with someone's kid," Latisha half-joked with him last week. Latisha is the head of product development who worked on the company's updated solar panels that will premiere at Zappzz.

Zappzz is the biggest energy conservation event of the year in the southeastern U.S. Alternative energy carriers, makers of energy-efficient products, environmental consulting firms, and even a few politicians and lobbyists attend.

To make headlines with a product or service being introduced at Zappzz is a major win.

You've just had your fifth contact with a method of lead generation, events, and trade shows.

Types of Leads

The variety of leads vary in name from industry to industry. However, there are some pretty universal lead types.

Types of leads include the following (Duggal, 2023).

- outbound leads

- inbound leads

- cold leads

- warm leads

- hot leads

- information-qualified leads

- marketing qualified leads

- sales-qualified leads

Outbound Leads

Recall our situation with the person from Company RST who is using the phone to contact companies about Company RST's windows? The person from Company RST is dialing the main phone number for a company and asking to speak with someone in the business development department. We described that as cold-calling, which is a type of outbound lead.

Outbound leads are defined by the direction the **initial** communication is flowing. When the business initiates the contact, they're choosing the time and mechanism of the message. Types of outbound leads include mass mailings, mass emails, physical circulars/flyers sent through the mail, and advertisements.

An Example of an Outbound Lead

Tech-X-Plo-Sion is an annual (and fictional) technology trade show and job fair held in Anycity in the U.S. Tech-X-Plo-Sion. The companies that attend are targeting individual customers and business customers.

Technology startup XYZ makes voice-controlled vacuum cleaning robots. XYZ does not think a technology tradeshow is an event that their potential customers would think of attending on their own. XYZ hires an advertising agency to create mailers for them, which they send to cleaning service firms located within 150 miles of Anycity. XYZ is hoping that the cleaning service firms will attend Tech-X-Plo-Sion and visit their booth, thus seeing their voice-controlled vacuum cleaning robot in action.

The Pros of Outbound Leads

- Control

Outbound leads allow the business to be in control of more factors. They decide what message to convey, how to convey it, and when to convey it. There is not any outside pressure.

- Brand Awareness

Outbound leads generate awareness of the business's brand. In our outbound lead example, a technology trade show is not an event that a professional cleaning service would find relevant. However, if they received a mailer from XYZ touting they'll be there with their voice-controlled vacuum cleaning robot, the professional cleaning service may send a couple of their employees to check out this innovative way of cleaning.

Quick Results

Outbound leads can bring quick results. Once the mailing (email, circular, flier) wings its way through the postal service, all it takes is one business to take note and make contact. Once they've gotten in touch, they're officially a potential customer!

The Cons of Outbound Leads

- Limited and Time-Consuming

Outbound leads are limited because of their reach. A sales representative employed by Company C is working through a list of companies who may (based on research done by Company C) be interested. Finding an interested party may take a lot of time.

"Didn't you just say that 'outbound leads can bring quick results'?" you ask. (We like that you're paying attention and that you care that we're consistent!)

Yes, we did list "quick results" as a positive aspect of outbound leads. Yes, they can bring quick results.

However, the person or business in receipt of your flier or your cold call has to have a preexisting interest in your product or service. The only way to find that out is to initiate the contact. Thus, a sales representative may call seven companies prior to finding an interested party, or the sales representative may have to call 70 companies.

- Burnout

Salespersons whose daily task it is to make cold calls may become frustrated after spending hours on the phone without generating a single lead. Also, not everyone who answers their call is polite or courteous. Rejection, especially when paired with rudeness or dismissiveness, can bring anyone down. That's not to say potential customers behave that way usually or are bad people; we're all human, and if having a bad day, we're apt to be short-tempered.

Sales representatives who call on other businesses in person have the added stress of being made to wait. Think of a pharmaceutical sales rep.

They may need to wait half an hour or hours before a doctor or medical professional can spare five minutes to speak with them.

Up next is the topic of inbound leads.

Inbound Leads

Remember the person from Company RST? They're using the phone, dialing the main phone number for a company, and asking to speak with someone in the business development department. Let's reconfigure the situation.

The person working for Company RST is sitting by the phone, and it rings. Someone is calling because they saw an online article about Company RST's windows.

With an inbound lead, an interested party chooses the method and time to contact a business with regard to something that interests them about the business's product or service.

Inbound leads are defined by the direction the **initial** communication is flowing. Unlike outbound leads, the communication involved with an inbound lead flows from an interested party to a business. To be more specific, with inbound leads, someone is reacting to the idea of your business's products or services.

The Pros of Inbound Leads

- Breadth

Inbound leads often result from a single effort. A business creates an advertisement, posts an article, or sets up an online form. Many potential customers may respond to the advertisement, article, or online form. The business only had to create each of those things one time. It's like taking out ten flocks of birds with one stone. To be more respectful of our animal friends, it's like cutting one hole in a net that contains a thousand fish. All the fish can exit through the single hole, as opposed to cutting a thousand discrete holes.

- Free Market Research

For each response to the advertisement, article, or online form, the business can learn a lot. They can see how many interested parties responded, within how much time they responded, from what industry they came from, etc. A business doesn't need to spend money on a market research tool in order to gather information on potential customers. Customer data is flowing freely to them via the responses.

The Cons of Inbound Leads

- Waiting for Results

Yes, inbound leads may come from a single effort. However, it may take a period of time from the point at which someone sees the advertisement, article, or online form to the point when someone reaches out to the business. Maybe the potential customer wants to do some research about the business or learn more about the product or service the business is offering before they reach out to the business.

- Less Control

With inbound leads, the business has less control over the situation. An interested party has to notice the advertisement, article, or online form. Then, they have to choose whether to respond to it, how to respond to it, and in what period of time. With outbound leads, the business initiates communication, and therefore, controls who they contact and when they make contact.

We're going to take a brief break from talking about lead types. We're going to share an example that demonstrates a tectonic shift in the way an industry approached selling. Our focus is the field of pharmaceutical sales. For decades, pharmaceutical sales relied on generating outbound leads. Then, COVID-19 happened.

Fresh From the Field: The Effect of COVID-19 on Pharmaceutical Sales

Unfortunately, we aren't talking about the latest farm-to-table special at a restaurant when we say, "Fresh from the field." We're making a play on words when talking about the sales field, but you knew that. We're trying to keep things fun...in a work-related sort of way.

Okay, back to the point. We are talking about the world of pharmaceutical sales.

With the established practice (known as "detailing") of commuting to a doctor's office or hospital in a crisp suit regardless of the weather, the typical route for pharmaceutical salespersons was disrupted with the onset of COVID-19. A patient's family member wasn't allowed to escort them to a chemotherapy appointment, so you're correct in thinking that cold-calling representatives were barred from oncology practices.

Pharmaceutical Companies Made Immediate Changes to Business Practices

According to an article published by FiercePharma in March 2020, they described the survey they created and the answers they received, noting the changes made by pharmaceutical companies (Snyder-Bulik, 2020).

"Bayer field staffers–including sales, market access, and medical teams–have all been asked to work from home until further notice" (Snyder-Bulik, 2o2o, paragraph 3).

"Pfizer customer-facing employees in the U.S. and Puerto Rico have switched to virtual customer tools to stay in contact with healthcare providers and others, " a Pfizer spokeswoman said. The company will reassess the decision as the situation changes." (Snyder-Bulik, 2020, paragraph 4).

"Sanofi said it is encouraging all office-based employees to work from home, which include field reps "who are expected to leverage digital tools and platforms in lieu of face-to-face meetings to interact with customers," a spokesperson said in an email." (Snyder-Bulik, 2020, paragraph 5).

"Novartis is asking all U.S. employees to work from home beginning Monday through at least April 3, with the caveat that "based on the nature of the work of some associates, it is not always feasible to work remotely–these associates will receive guidance specific to their role from their local leadership teams," according to a spokesperson" (Snyder-Bulik, 2020, paragraph 5).

GlaxoSmithKline, Merck, Bristol Myers Squibb, Johnson & Johnson, Global Blood Therapeutics, and Biogen were also a part of the study (Snyder-Bulik, 2o2o).

Put yourself in the place of these sales reps, who learned and then mastered outbound selling techniques. Now, the means and medium for your day-to-day job are stalled indefinitely. Commensurate with the rest of the world, whose livelihoods were conducted outside of the four walls in which they lived, pharmaceutical salespersons scrambled to come up with a way to generate sales leads when they couldn't go out!

An Effect of the Changes Implemented by Pharmaceutical Companies

McKinsey & Company reviewed the Sermo COVID-19 Healthcare Practitioner Survey, dated April of 2020. The survey tabulated the number of in-person consultations between healthcare professionals and pharmaceutical representatives over a six-month period, from approximately October 2019 through March 2020. At the beginning of the six-month period, pharmaceutical representatives across multiple drug types conducted approximately 80 visits per week; at the time of the survey, pharmaceutical representatives conducted less than five visits per week (Cohen, Fox, Mills, and Wright, n.d.)

Around the world, challenges like supply chain delays and increased demand for medications further flummoxed the flailing pharmaceutical industry.

Pharmaceutical Companies' Top Two Priorities

Two of the top priorities for pharma companies' commercial organizations must be to ensure the ongoing delivery of consistent supply and access to drugs and of high-quality patient care and to safeguard their employees. After triaging the priorities, commercial-pharma leaders can shift their focus on bouncing back from the crisis. They will need to navigate through the muddled and uncharted territory of recovery from a global pandemic. Points to weigh heavily include dedicated attention to customer concerns that may not have been in existence prior to the pandemic.

While the consistent flow of necessary drugs to patients, patient care, and employee safety was the first and foremost concern, pharmaceutical companies had to move quickly to look at the commercial implications, including how they sell and manage revenue. If the phrase "profit over people (Chomsky and Mcchesney, 2011)" bounced around in your brain, we challenge you to consider what would happen if pharmaceutical firms did not think hard about sales practices and revenue. Without sales, there is no revenue, without revenue, there is no money with which to continue to provide life-saving medications or to develop new ones.

The Evolving Landscape of Pharmaceutical Sales

Pharmaceutical companies asked many questions as the lockdowns abated.

- How do we re-engage with our customers (e.g., medical professionals and patients)?

- What ways can we rely on to conduct market intelligence, which will drive re-engagement?

- When countries and regions become more physically accessible, how do we handle the uneven demand?

McKinsey & Company directed their pharmaceutical customers towards practices that addressed the "new normal."

- Study, address, and communicate the effects of existing drugs with COVID-19.

- Shift towards technology and digital processes to work with customers. Virtual events and remote learning are two examples.

- Increase the speed at which messages and materials are dispersed to medical staff and patients. As the situations surrounding COVID-19 evolve, so must the means of customer education and support. Examples include offering medical webinars on the latest data and multi-customer video conferences during which treatment protocols are discussed.

The Economic Impacts of COVID-19 on the Pharmaceutical Sector

Many of the pharmaceutical majors, in reporting their second-quarter (2020) and first-half (2020) results, showed some effect of declining revenues year-over-year attributable to the COVID-19 pandemic (Van Arnum, 2020).

Pfizer reported revenues of $11.8 billion and $23.8 billion for the first half of 2020, respectively, an 11% and 10% decline (Van Arnum, 2020). Pfizer credited the decrease in revenue to a drop in in-person engagement between their salesforce and physicians. Also negatively affecting revenue, there was a decline in prescriptions.

Bristol Myers Squibb's revenue remained consistent on a pro forma basis, as sales were estimated to be negatively impacted by approximately $600 million due mainly to COVID-19-related channel inventory work-downs from the first quarter (Van Arnum, 2020). However, unlike Pfizer, Bristol Myers Squibb credited the decline to fewer new patients starting medications and fewer patient visits to physicians.

Contrary to the decrease in revenue observed as an effect of COVID-19, pharmaceutical company Amgen reported a total revenue increase for the second quarter of 2020. Amgen reported that its total revenues increased 6% to $6.2 billion in the second quarter of 2020 in comparison to the second quarter of 2019, driven by higher unit demand and offset partially by lower net selling prices (Van Arnum, 2020).

Closing

As with many of the effects of COVID-19, we won't know the long-term impacts for many years. Pharmaceutical sales, especially given the nature of their long-established practices with outbound leads, will continue to pivot, redirect, and grow.

Cold Leads

We're going to revisit our RST Company employee for a final time. Tasked with calling a list of companies and hoping to make contact with someone who would respond with "Yes, we're interested in the windows you're selling" is an accurate portrayal of a cold lead.

Let's assume the RST Company employee researched the companies before he called them. Presumably, he would not be calling a business that lacked windows (e.g., a mobile food truck, on which the only glass was in the windshield).

Other than the "no need for windows" qualifier, the RST Company employee was calling any and all businesses within a specified geographic territory. He had no indication if the business he was contacting was interested in new windows or if they knew about RST Company.

Cold leads are the most challenging type of leads to convert to customers. There is no way for a sales representative to tell if the business they're contacting has a need for the product or service.

Warm Leads

Unsurprisingly, warm leads are the middle ground between cold leads and hot leads. If you're a fan of the television series *Star Trek: The Next Generation*, warm leads are the sales territory equivalent of the neutral zone.

Some professional organizations classify warm leads as a type of inbound lead. Some drop them directly into the cold lead category. We are going to stick with describing them, and then you can classify them as you wish.

An individual or company that has shown interest in your business is a warm lead. Maybe they are frequent readers of your blog. They're aware of what you do, are familiar with your brand, or perhaps a representative from your business spoke with them at an event.

Warm leads are easier to work with as there is some level of interest already established.

An Example of a Warm Lead

Let's look at a fictional example of a warm lead. If you're not in the financial services or investment management space, we're going to make this extra interesting for you by creating the warm lead scenario in the world of banking.

We'll start with a quick background on a type of trading.

Fun Financial Fact

Margin trading refers to the practice of using borrowed funds from a broker to trade a financial asset, which forms the collateral for the loan from the broker (Fernando, 2022). Said simply, if you're trading on margin, you're using your own money, and you're borrowing money from a broker in order to trade a type of financial asset (e.g., stocks).

A Warm Lead at Work

Marge is a fictional software solutions company that creates applications for margin trading. Unlike Marge, margin trading is a real thing.

Along with other trading operations software suppliers, Marge sends representatives (Jasper and Jillian) to conferences attended by financial institutions. Sooper Money is the largest conference of its type, drawing investment professionals representing financial companies from all over the world.

Naturally, Jasper and Jillian represent Marge at Sooper Money. On the second day at Sooper Money, Jillian has a conversation with a Bankz Bank representative, Alan. Alan is the technology manager responsible for trading operations at Bankz Bank.

Alan explains that Bankz Bank may be looking for an initial margin (IM) software module. Alan continues to explain that Bankz Bank may or may not be (Alan holds a Juris Doctor (JD) and understands every line of the confidentiality agreement he signed as part of his employment contract with Bankz Bank) using a homegrown system that is at capacity in terms of volume.

After Sooper Money concludes, the Marge representatives return home. The first day they are back in the office, Jillian telephones Alan at Bankz Bank to discuss the IM solution he may or may not have been interested in learning about.

At Sooper Money, Alan already indicated he may be interested in an IM software solution. While Jillian initiated the follow-up contact, she knew Bankz Bank was interested already.

Hot Leads

With a hot lead, an interested party has demonstrated a concrete interest in a business's products or services. The interested party may have completed an online survey created by the business, maybe they have requested a demonstration of the business's product, or an individual from the interested party has contacted the business directly.

Three aspects that accompany hot leads include:

1. The interested party has a problem to which the business can provide a solution.

2. Someone with authority or in a decision-making role within the interested party is communicating with the business.

3. The interested party is within the business's target market.

An Example of Two Types of Leads: An Inbound Lead and A Hot Lead

Let's revisit and rework the warm lead example to demonstrate an inbound lead and a hot lead.

Instead of conversing with Jillian about a hypothetical interest in an IM solution, Alan of Bankz Bank was ready to move on the IM solution.

Alan shared his electronic business card with Jillian. Next, he asked her to set up a date and time for a telephone conversation to talk about the operating system on which the IM solution runs. Then, Alan requested that Jillian invite one of Marge's original developers involved in the creation of the IM solution to participate in the call. Alan explained that he was going to have a trade operations analyst from Bankz Bank participate in the call. Finally, ever the JD, Alan confirmed Jillian's email address in order to send softcopies of a mutual non-disclosure agreement to her with expectations everyone involved in the forthcoming call will have signed them.

These actions comprise an inbound and a hot lead instead of a warm lead. If you want to be certain about determining whether it is an inbound lead or a hot lead, check what you know about them against the situation.

The Direction of the Initial Communication Flow

Which way is the communication flowing? Alan from Bankz Bank shared his electronic business card with Jillian from Marge. Alan asked about having a teleconference with Jillian. As you can see, Alan is leading the communication and initiating interaction beyond the present conversation. That's two indicators of the lead being inbound in nature.

The Three Aspects that Make It Hot

How do you know it's a hot lead?

1. Bankz Bank's homegrown technology that currently supports trading on initial margin might not be able to handle the volumes of trades coming through it. That's a problem that Marge can solve. Bankz Bank would not go to a business consulting firm to solve the problem. Business consultants may be able to assist in sourcing a good IM solution, but they don't provide it.

2. Alan is the head of trading operations and applications at Bankz Bank. Presumably, he has the authority to select the technology for which he is responsible.

3. Marge is a software solutions company, and Bankz Bank is a financial institution. Banks, investment managers, financial institutions, and high-net-worth individuals are interested in software solutions that deal with initial margin. It sounds like a fit. Yoga enthusiasts and venture capitalists probably would not be interested in Marge's offerings.

Information-Qualified Leads

An information-qualified lead originates with an individual or a company when they actively start seeking a solution to solve a problem or improve their existing status quo.

Consider the following situation: A business consulting firm, Len & Lean, posts on their blog, advertising an upcoming webinar on lean manufacturing practices. Within the post is a link to click to indicate interest in viewing the webinar. The link redirects to an online form with fields in which one enters their contact information to be enrolled in the webinar.

Information-qualified leads benefit the business as the business knows there is a pre-existing level of interest in their product or service. They don't have to dig to find out if an interest exists. That saves time, effort, and frustration.

Businesses can make the most of information-qualified leads in three ways.

1. When the sales representative from the business gets in touch with the contact person, one of the first things they should find out is what prompted the contact person's interest in the business. Is the contact person's company considering putting out a Request for Proposal (RFP)? Do they plan to solicit bids for a project?

2. The sales representative should provide the contact person with relevant information on the product or service in which they showed interest. We're not talking about forwarding softcopies of the standard product literature to them. We're talking about sending information connected to the contact person's specific interest.

3. Learn as much about the contact's company as possible. Discover what the company is about, how it originated, and who their target markets are. Scan the news headlines of business or trade journals. Does the company hold patents? Has the company won awards? Does it take social responsibility seriously (e.g., do they practice sustainable sourcing, do they promote diversity and inclusion, how do they care for the

Earth?)

Earth?)

An Example of an Information-Qualified Lead

Len & Lean can study the information input by the contact persons who completed the online form indicating their interest in the lean manufacturing processes webinar.

After studying the information, Len & Lean knows more about the companies interested in the webinar. For specificity's sake, let's assume they've learned that most of the companies operate within the automotive industry. From that point, Len & Lean may choose to send emails to the contacts, including additional information on the upcoming webinar.

In addition to the link to the webinar, conference call bridge number, and access code, Len & Lean might attach an FAQ for lean manufacturing process trends that have been noted within the industry. Alternatively, they might include a case study about the notable efficiency gains that lean manufacturing processes have facilitated within the automotive industry.

Marketing-Qualified Leads

A marketing-qualified lead is an information-qualified lead that evolved. Interested parties that are marketing qualified leads are taking greater measures to examine a specific business's products and services. They're doing more than showing a casual interest in a topic; they're looking for how a specific business addresses the topic.

Continuing to work with our business consulting firm, let's fast forward to the period after the webinar concludes.

An Example of a Marketing Qualified Lead

Len & Lean reviews the logs of the webinar attendees. The logs indicate when each participant joined and how long they were viewing the webinar. The logs also indicate if the participant asked any questions and what the questions were.

Len & Lean concludes that anyone that viewed the webinar has a particular interest in how they approach lean manufacturing. The webinar was three hours and forty-seven minutes in length; even if you live and breathe for running an efficient plant, that is a serious commitment.

Sales-Ready Leads

For a lead to be considered sales-ready, the interested party has their proverbial "ducks in a row." The interested party evaluated the business's product or service in light of budgeting, decision-making, solution-seeking, and urgency.

Budgeting

From a budget standpoint, the interested party knows the costs involved with a business's product or service. They know the minimum, average, and maximum price tags attached. They and the business have reviewed the cost drivers and estimated a margin for "scope creep" (when the parameters of what is needed to grow, along with the cost). It's likely that the interested party has involved their finance and sourcing departments to be ready to examine the pending expenditure and contractual obligations, respectively.

Decision-Making

Within the interested party's organization, a decision-maker is usually involved in teleconferences and meetings by this point. Depending on the cost, the decision-maker may be a department head, managing director, or vice president. Each company is set up differently, even within the same industry. It isn't so much the person's title that matters, it is whether the potential customer has a decision-maker engaged.

Solution-Seeking

The interested party should have discussed an existing problem that the business's product or service will address. The existing problem usually is well-defined at this point in the timeline, and possibly the interested party is looking at other providers, too.

If the existing problem is described as "We want to reduce waste in our factories," that's too broad to be considered part of a sales-ready lead. In the sales-ready phase, a problem should be clearly defined, have pain points identified, and have target metrics included in the goal.

A sales-ready problem is described as "We want to reduce the amount of water we use in our denim-making processes that occur in our North American factories by 30% by the end of 2024. Our current consumption of water for these processes in the existing North American factories is costing too much and is environmentally wasteful as companies of similar size use 25% of the water we do."

- The pain points that exist in the current situation are expense and environmental unfriendliness: "Our current consumption of water for these processes in the existing North American factories is costing too much and is environmentally wasteful as companies of similar size use 25% of the water we do."

- The problem is clearly defined: "We want to use 30% less water during our denim-making processes that occur within our North American factories."

- There are target metrics: "We want to reduce the water we use by 30% in our North American factories by 2024."

Urgency

For the interested party to be active as a sales-ready lead, they should have a timeframe or date in mind for committing to the business's product or service. Unknown factors can throw off schedules and cause delays at any phase of a project. However, there should be a timeline and concrete dates set as parts of the discussions between the interested party and the business.

An Example of a Sales-Ready Lead

Len & Lean and their webinar on the topic of lean manufacturing will give us an example of a sales-ready lead.

After reviewing the logs from the webinar, Elizabeth (who works in sales support at Len & Lean) notes that one participant asked three questions and requested that Len & Lean contact them. The participant is Jake Brake, and he works at the car manufacturing company Fesla Tusk.

Via email, Elizabeth and Jake arrange a call to discuss the status quo at Fesla Tusk. During the call, Jake explains that they've had two internal efforts to streamline the processes on the factory floor. Neither has succeeded.

Elizabeth asks for Jake's assessment of the failures. Jake says that Fesla Tusk has engineers and people working on the line that have significant knowledge of the processes but very little time outside of their day job to write ideas down and test them out. Trying something new on a busy factory floor could result in accidents, plus they aren't allowed to deviate from the existing practices. Fesla Tusk also employs business strategists and analysts, but they lack the in-real-life experience of working on a line or under a hood.

The catalyst for reaching out to Len & Lean was a deal percolating between Fesla Tusk and the transportation authority in a major U.S. city. The transportation authority wants to pilot a program utilizing Fesla Tusk cars. Unless Fesla Tusk can reduce the time it takes to produce a vehicle, they will not be able to move forward with the deal.

Elizabeth tells Jake about the talents at Len & Lean. Many of their consultants have come up through manufacturing, some even from the automotive sector. Several business and financial analysts work at Len

& Lean, too. Within the company, consultants are paired with analysts based on similar experience and time in the field. A Len & Lean team is assigned to a client, and they work jointly with the client's employees.

Jake really likes the way Len & Lean teams are configured and learned several new facts from the webinar. He arranges an in-person meeting for himself and the vice president of operations of Fesla Tusk with Elizabeth and a consulting/analyst team from Len & Lean.

The meeting agenda includes:

- discussion of Fesla Tusk's pain points (e.g., the time it takes to manufacture a Tesla Fusk automobile)

- an expense review with the vice president of operations

- an estimation of project costs with a Len & Lean financial analyst

- review scrubbed case studies that highlight Len & Lean's success with other automotive manufacturers

- timeline for Len & Lean to complete their assessment and launch a collaboration with Fesla Tusk

After the meeting, the vice president of operations and Jake request a softcopy of Len & Lean's services agreement. They will send the services agreement to their global sourcing group and their legal counsel for review. Elizabeth and Jake set up another call for a week from that day to discuss the next steps.

The Fesla Tusk opportunity meets the criteria for a sales-ready lead.

- Budgeting: there are two separate discussions about expenses and project costs.

- Decision-making: the vice president of operations from Tesla Fusk is involved. They have the authority to approve an engagement with Len & Lean.

- Solution-seeking: Fesla Tusk's automobile-making processes are too slow.

- Urgency: Fesla Tusk will not be able to move forward with the pending deal with the transportation authority of a major U.S. city unless they can make cars faster. To make cars faster, they need to be efficient. Len & Lean offers consulting to accomplish this goal.

A Last Word

Your toolbox is continuing to fill. You know what lead generation is and why it matters. You've seen firsthand how frequently lead generation touches your daily life; we counted five examples in a 24-hour period! Know that whenever "Sales" is a topic in an upcoming television game show, you can name seven types of leads!

We brought the L2RM process to life with Sheldon, Megan, and a fictional home improvement store, HHS. We dug into the method of lead generation known as SEO with Delaney as she and her colleague discussed an upcoming meeting. Multiple aspects of lead generation came to life through fictional sequences featuring vacuum cleaning robots, pitching solar panels at an energy conference, and reviewing a meeting agenda written in the early phase of an initial margin software deal.

In Chapter One, we've ventured beyond academic understanding and fun fictional examples as we entered the real world. We've observed how a major clothing retailer works with qualifying leads when we visited Lululemon. We've taken a close look at a significant shift in selling methods as we examined COVID-19 and its implications for the pharmaceutical industry.

It's worth mentioning that Chapter One went into some high-level detail about some of the material covered in the upcoming chapters. As we did in the Introduction, we are presenting L2RM holistically; each part is separate and yet works together as parts of a whole.

Chapter Two

Lead Nurturing and Conversion

What Lead Nurturing and Lead Conversion Are

What is lead nurturing, and why should you care? Is lead conversion separate?

What it is: Lead nurturing is the process of developing a relationship with potential customers. Lead conversion is the process of turning a potential customer into a paying customer. Nurturing and conversion work together as a hand with a glove, peanut butter with jelly, and a fishing rod and reel.

Why you should care: Lead nurturing is important because it allows businesses to build relationships with potential customers and increase the chances of converting them into paying customers. By providing valuable, high-quality content and engaging meaningfully with potential customers, they are more likely to become paying customers. Without tending to potential customers, they may never become paying customers. Without paying customers, revenue falls, and without revenue, a business fails.

What You May Think Lead Nurturing and Conversion Are

If you work in one of these departments—sales, sales support, marketing, public relations, or business development—you have a good idea of what lead nurturing and conversion are. It's likely you make multiple contacts throughout the day, helping with the two processes.

Sales and Sales Support

If you're a sales representative, you contribute to the lead nurturing and conversion processes by following up with a potential customer (we'll call them "Prospect M.") whom you may have met at a trade show. The follow-up could be via a telephone call or an email, very briefly touching on a conversation you had when Prospect M visited your company's booth. If you're in sales support, you may work directly with a sales representative. You may help her by documenting her interactions with Prospect M in the CRM database. Your accurate recording of the sales representative's interactions is key to helping the rep stay organized when it comes to her dealings with Prospect M.

Marketing

As a marketer, your role with nurturing and conversion may be from a strategic perspective. Perhaps you're checking the sales pipeline and seeing where Prospect M fits into the company's overall marketing goals. You might enlighten the sales representative about some upcoming conferences at which your company will be presenting that Prospect M may want to attend.

Public Relations

If you work within public relations, you will be sure to have flagged the sales representative's attention to an upcoming press release about the product in which Prospect M is interested. You'll remind the rep of the date it will be published and the approximate time the story is released.

Business Development

Inside the business development realm, you're paying close attention to who the prospects are and what they want from your company's products. If Prospect M's focus is on a product that is trending with many other prospects, you'll ensure your senior management knows about it to encourage spending on research and development for this product.

The Support Roles Within Lead Nurturing and Conversion

That list of roles may not surprise you at all. Are you aware of the other business functions that touch lead nurturing and conversion?

You mean outside the ones listed, you're musing.

Yes, there are other parts of the business that affect lead nurturing and conversion. They may not be as obvious, but they are there.

Customer Support

If a prospect or a prospect's company has questions about the product it is assessing, they may call customer support rather than calling the sales representative. Especially if the product is technical in nature, the assumption might be that a question is best fielded by the people who answer product questions all day and every day.

Customer support can be a daunting job. We empathize. It's hard to keep a smile in your voice and your eyes from rolling back into your head (permanently). Each day may challenge your mantra that there are no such things as dumb questions. However, every call that comes in may not be from an existing customer.

Some of the communication can come from individuals that are almost interested. Thus, we gently encourage you to "flip your script." Instead of hearing a question that really pushes the truth behind "there are no such things as dumb questions," think of the question asker as someone who is uninformed, and you're helping them. They're uninformed because they lack part of the story, not because they're idiots. We bet that even Albert Einstein and Marie Curie asked questions in order to learn about their subjects.

Administrative Personnel

When you were a child, perhaps you had a role in a play or a musical performance. Maybe you had recurring roles as a townsperson or a nameless heckler in a swarm of naysayers. Your parents or guardians might have consoled you by saying, "There are no small parts" when it comes to telling a story.

The same is true when it comes to lead nurturing and conversion. If you work in the building, you have a role. This applies especially to those who work as personal assistants, secretaries, interoffice-mail deliverers, and custodial personnel. Often, you are the first face a prospect sees when they come through the door. What you're saying and how you're saying it matters because you are overheard. You may be the first person a prospect approaches. Maybe they have a question or need to be directed to someone in the sales department. People tend to remember first impressions, and you might be the one they recall.

An In-Depth Look at Lead Nurturing and Conversion

It is a rare situation when an interested party has one interaction with a business that leads to a single touch point that leads to a sale.

By "touch point," we mean small interactions such as the interested party requesting a white paper written by the business or sending an email after they've participated in a webinar led by the business. Other touch points may include visiting the business's physical location for a meet-and-greet or seeking out the business at an event or trade show.

Lead nurturing is a bit like finding a partner and committing to one person. Most people who are single meet another individual who is single. If there is an interest, then there are other interactions that help to build awareness of each other. Texts, phone calls, Zoom meetings, going places together, etc., forge the foundation of a relationship long before a commitment is formed. In this example, lead conversion is parallel to a marriage or civil union.

The Importance of Lead Nurturing

A Scary Statistic

According to Invesp, a shocking 80 percent of new leads never convert into sales (Kelwig, 2023).

Reread that, please, and let it sink in for a moment. Now, picture what that looks like.

You start with 100 new leads. You talk with them, send them relevant emails, interact with them at events, and ensure they have information about your business's offerings at their fingertips. If you're the type to go the extra mile, you might have made a mental note of where a business contact's child goes to college or where her husband likes to fish. You sprinkle these facts into the conversation when speaking with her, knowing that retaining the information won't close a $20 million software deal, but it is one of the tiny positive interactions that build a relationship.

After weeks or months of those actions (all of which involve time, resources, and possibly sticky notes), only 20 of them will convert to sales.

In baseball, that is a .200 batting average. To those who know the sport, they know that this is well below average. It's a well-known benchmark, titled the "Mendoza Line." Fun fact: The origin story of the Mendoza Line traces back to the late 1970s in the Pacific Northwest in the city of Seattle. Mario Mendoza's teammates began poking at him about his batting average because he fought to keep or achieve a .200 average (Bailey, 2022).

In fitness (and many other areas), the phrase "the 80/20 rule" is cited when it comes to sticking to healthy eating and exercise. Within the bounds of the 80/20 rule, 80% of the time, one should enjoy whole foods and avoid processed foods. Applying that rule to exercise, one should be active 80% of the time. Following the 80/20 rule, processed foods and couch-dwelling are acceptable 20% of the time.

Paralleling baseball and fitness with sales lead conversion, converting 20% of leads is the equivalent of a below-mediocre batting average, coupled with chips and sofa-snoozing. Those are not exactly ringing endorsements, are they?

How Do We Counteract the Statistic?

So, what should one do to increase sales leads into sales conversions?

This is where the practice of lead nurturing comes into play.

Lead nurturing is important because it gives businesses the chance to increase that 20%. What was that we mentioned earlier? Lead nurturing was based on providing valuable content to a prospect and meaningful engagement with the prospect.

How does a business provide valuable content and meaningful engagement? We hope you're asking the same thing.

Methods of Lead Nurturing

Lead nurturing can be done in an assortment of ways. However, before we get into the specific methods of lead nurturing, we want to run something by you.

We guarantee you have been a lead that has been nurtured. Perhaps you didn't notice!

Does this scenario sound familiar?

A Simple Example of Nurturing a Lead

You see an online article about the evolution of food delivery services. Within the article is a link to a snack box delivery website which piques your interest to the point where you click on the link. Once the page loads, you see the snack box delivery service offers a free trial box of goodies once you sign up to receive the company's emails.

Recalling your child's recriminations of "there's never any good snacks here," you type in your name and email address, secure in the knowledge that a box of tasty treats will be winging its way to you in 7–10 business days. Just like that, you went from being a cold lead to being a warm lead, to becoming a nurtured lead.

Let's walk through your evolution.

1. First, you saw an article about food delivery services. You're a cold lead at this point. You're just one of millions sailing through cyberspace.

2. Second, you saw a link to a website that advertised itself as a snack box deliverer. You are interested (or you are hungry). You point and click. You've heated up to the degree of a warm lead.

3. Third, you read about the availability of a free snack box, with the entry of your name and email. You complete the online form and are eagerly awaiting your snacks. The snack box service nurtured your lead once you were interested enough to click on the link to their site.

And… Converting a Lead

You know the scene in a horror movie when a guy sees the basement door hanging open (usually creaking) and starts walking toward it? You know what is going to happen. The poor guy isn't long for this world, as a maniac wearing a Calliou mask lurks deep in the basement shadows, ready to chop him into bits to mail to his relatives.

If we were to tell a bystander to add a fourth point to the snack box example above, the bystander would add a point involving lead conversion.

After you enjoy your box of free munchies (well, what is left of it after your child raids it), you sign up and pay for a monthly delivery of a snack box. There you go; you're a converted lead.

It's worth noting that this example is purposefully simple, and most business-to-business transactions are much more complicated. The premise remains the same. Once someone (or a company) shows an interest, a business will want to cultivate the interest as a way of building a relationship that leads to a converted sale.

Ways to Nurture Leads

We're going to examine six methods.

1. Personalization

The first one is personalization. This method is seen in business-to-consumer lead nurturing. If you've ever been shopping in a cosmetics and skincare store, such as Sephora or Ulta, you may have seen signage advertising products for various types of skin concerns.

"Do you have oily skin?"

"Are you bothered by patches of dryness?"

"Have lines and wrinkles started forming?"

The aforesaid questions often are posed in advertising materials for skincare. Some skincare companies take the questions to a personal level by inviting people to take an online quiz or download their app to access a skin wellness Q&A. By inputting answers to the questions in the online (or in-app) form, the skincare company learns about your unique concerns. After you complete the quiz, a list of results and suggestions appears.

Fragrances often use quizzes to help a person determine what perfume they'd like.

"What is the most appealing environment?"

- Winds sweep across an empty beach just before a rainstorm.

- A shopkeeper opens the window of her flower shop in Provence, France.

- It's midafternoon in a souk, and the tea makers are brewing chai.

- A pine forest is lit only by the moon, reflecting on the new-fallen snow.

"If you selected the first one, your fragrance type is fresh, aquatic, and crisp. Your perfume match is C."

"If you selected the second one, your fragrance crush is nothing but flowers. Your perfume match is D."

"If you selected the third one, you're spicy at heart and like to radiate warmth. Your perfume match is E."

"If you selected the fourth one, you would feel most at home with woodsy, green scents. Your perfume match is F."

Not coincidentally, scents C through F are sold by the perfume maker who generated the quiz.

2. Call To Action

A call to action (CTA) is giving guidance or encouragement to a prospect. CTAs can take the form of emails, banners on websites, and statements on the back of promotional items.

In a business-to-business situation, a CTA might be attached to a promotional item. At a tradeshow for iron and steel companies, a vendor, Best ERP, Inc., is handing out tiny hammers with a tag attached, exhorting, "Contact us to hammer out your next Enterprise Resource Planning (ERP) software solution!"

In another business-to-business solution, a CTA found on an information management website might be targeted at healthcare administrators (i.e., the non-clinical side of the medical profession, such as patient records and patient billing). The CTA might ask a question, such as, "Are you still dealing with the headaches of paper files? Contact us today for a demo of our cutting-edge patient information management system, PIMs!"

3. Lead Scoring

It's time to get quantitative. As in, we're going to inject some numbers into our study of lead nurturing and conversion.

A Brief Word About Numbers

Please note, if you don't like math or would rather leave the number-crunching to someone else, that's fine…most of the time. The beauty of math and numbers is that they have one answer.

Imagine you and your mom are visiting the Royal Garden Party. You're looking at a row of six pots of roses. Your mom says, "They're beautiful." You dislike roses and tell her, "They're not beautiful." If your mom tells you there are six pots, no matter how much you dislike them, there are six pots of roses. It's an irrefutable statement.

The point is that it is wise to recognize the importance numbers and math can play, especially when it comes to supporting facts and statements. Said differently, including some numerical data points in your argument gives you a winning edge. Now we have your attention, right?

Lead scoring is a method of assigning a score to each lead based on their level of engagement and interest. This allows businesses to prioritize leads and focus their efforts on the most promising leads.

Prioritizing happens all the time, in the business world and outside of it. If you've ever been to a hospital accident and emergency (A&E) department or an emergency room (ER), you know that someone with a twisted ankle won't be seen by the medical staff before someone with a drooping facial expression accompanied by numb limbs (usually signs of a heart attack). In healthcare, it's referred to as "triage." In the L2RM world, it's known as prioritization and quantified through lead scoring.

You can score your leads based on a variety of factors, including the professional information they've submitted to you and how they've interacted with your website and your company's brand across the internet (Kolowich-Cox, 2022).

According to a blog post by Hubspot, "Lead Scoring 101: How to Use Data to Calculate a Basic Lead Score," there are six types of information that can be evaluated when scoring leads (Kolowich-Cox, 2022). The six are demographics, behavior, level of email engagement, level of social engagement, business profile, and spam detection (Kolowich-Cox, 2022). Spam detection is the only type of information that rules a lead out instead of includes a lead.

Demographic Information

Demographic information includes attributes like gender, age, geography, and rank. A lead scoring method that considers demographic information will assign higher numbers to leads that fit certain demographic attributes and lower numbers to leads that don't have certain demographic attributes.

Behavioral Information

Behavioral information usually refers to online behavior. How is the online behavior observed? This is where web analytics comes into play.

A business utilizing a web analytics tool collects data points about users' online behavior.

For a household goods retailer, they may use web analytics to determine how many users click on coupons and spend a certain amount of money. For example, once this type of information is gathered, business analysts evaluate one fact (e.g., a user clicks on a coupon) in context with another fact (e.g., a user purchases more than $100 in a single transaction). With enough data points collected, the business can tell whether there is a link between users who click on coupons and their propensity to spend $100 or more. The business can assign a lead score to the act of offering online coupons. Of course, this type of lead scoring varies a bit from assigning a score to lead, as it assigns a score to an action taken by many leads.

Email Engagement and Social Engagement

We will pair these two together. Monitoring the company contact recipients who open an email from your business can indicate which company contacts should be assigned a higher lead score. A higher lead score may mean that you make a telephone call to the company contact.

Social engagement is tracking the way people interact with a business's social media platform. Again, using the company contact example, if a business's web analytics tool can show which company contacts comment on the business's blog posts or "like" the business's posts, the business can assign higher lead scores to those company contacts.

Business Profile Information

The business profile for a company conveys information that is relevant to business-to-business commerce. Business profile information may determine if the company being assessed for its lead potential earns a higher or lower score, assuming the lead scoring system is meant to target specific types of businesses. Types of businesses may be based on headcount, industry, or years the business has operated.

Spam Detection

This type of lead scoring flies in the face of every motivational poster, suggesting one should "Focus on the Positive!" Lead scoring can assign a negative value to leads that may be false.

How would a business know a lead might be false, just based on how a lead fills out an online form? If you are an analyst within a business and you are reviewing form data, you may notice things like a lowercase letter starting a first name or six digits in the telephone field (most telephone numbers are seven or ten digits, depending on whether a country code is included). Since most names start with a capital letter, one that starts with a lowercase letter raises a red flag. Likewise, a six-digit telephone number seems suspicious due to its lack of length.

4. Lead Magnets

Lead magnets are items or offers of service that draw prospects to expand their dealings with a business or cement a sale. We've talked a lot about one lead magnet, which is the webinar. Free trials are an example of a service offering that may cement a sale.

As an unconventional example of a free trial, we refer you to an event that happened within the fiction book *The Magician's Assistant*. Parsifal, the titular magician, owned a rug store. Parsifal and his assistant, Sabine, traveled around the world buying rugs to sell at the store. There were prospects that came into the store to shop and were curious about a rug but unsure of committing to the expenditure. They were not $19.99 bathroom shag rugs that snuggled the base of a toilet; these rugs (e.g., Ladik) were worth thousands of dollars. Parsifal's deputized manager, Salvio, allowed the rug to be loaned to a customer who wanted to try it out in their home to see how it looked rather than guess how it might look. More often than not, the loan turned into a purchase.

5. Retargeting

As the name suggests, retargeting is making contact again with a prospective customer. The purpose is to remind the individual or company of the products and services of the business, which they already discussed at an earlier point in time.

Remember the earlier example with the software solutions vendor, Best ERP, Inc., distributing miniature hammers to iron and steel manufacturers? The miniature hammers included an exhortation to "Contact us to hammer out your next Enterprise Resource Planning (ERP) software solution!"

Should Best ERP, Inc. want to use retargeting, they may send out an email to those companies that gave their contact information. The email might include an image of a hammer with the question, "Since we met, have you hammered out your next ERP solution?"

6. Customer Relationship Management (CRM)

If you're a seasoned sales support person or sales representative, you may laugh a bit at the idea of CRM being unique to lead nurturing. You might say, "CRM is a full-time job!"

You would be right, of course. However, used in this context, CRM is a useful resource, especially for the lead nurturing phase. We will caveat that with a follow-up statement that "CRM is only as useful as its users." A good CRM system allows a story to be told for each prospective customer.

What story? *Aren't we supposed to be telling the truth*? you wonder. Who contributes to the story? What makes it "good?"

The journey from cold lead to interested party to prospect to serious prospect to customer is a unique journey for every client. We're referring to it as a story.

Some stories are simple and brief; the business meets a representative from a company at an event, and the representative requests information, becoming an interested party. From that point, there is a meeting or two before conversion is complete.

Other stories are complex and Odysseyian in length (If you didn't read or study Classics at your university or college, maybe you read a poem or two in the sixth form or as a senior in high school. The Odyssey is a poem comprising 24 books.). There may be a deal brokered in the after-hours of a tradeshow between two senior vice presidents, one who represents a potential supplier and one who represents a potential buyer. The vice presidents deputize their respective departments to make it official. Oh, and they expect it to be official in three weeks. There's one more thing; the buying company already put out an RFP…a month ago. Oh, and one last tiny detail, the potential supplier is in the final stages of a merger with another supplier that happened to respond to the buyer company's RFP.

Anyone who interacts with the prospect is an author. The quality of a story depends on the level of detail each author enters. The usefulness of each story depends on the reader and the frequency with which they read the entries about a prospective customer.

Assume that the sales support person, Judd Miles, makes the first cold call and diligently records the interaction (e.g., "March 29, 2023: J. Miles spoke with the business development manager at Splendid Steel, Inc. They're going to put out an RFP for a new ERP system in the fourth quarter.")

The sales support person knows that he should wait until early May to follow-up for a second time, based on the information he entered. They won't be issuing an RFP for a new ERP system until the fourth quarter. A call placed in early May will remind Splendid Steel of Best ERP, Inc.'s interest.

A Last Word

Lead nurturing is a vital prerequisite to lead conversion, as we've discovered. In addition to the usual suspects (e.g., sales managers) involved in cultivating a prospect's interest, there are others (e.g., front office personnel) within the business that impact the lead nurturing process. There are a variety of lead nurturing methods, which may be as creative as using mini-tools as giveaway items (e.g., a CTA) or as gray as a prioritization scorecard (e.g., lead scoring).

As we move into the next chapter focused on lead management and tracking, you'll see just how interconnected lead generation, nurturing, and conversion are. The three steps cement themselves as building blocks for successful lead management, which is critically important. Equally important is lead tracking since lead management is not a "one-and-done" activity and requires recurring follow-up that needs to be measured.

Chapter Three

Lead Management & Tracking

What Lead Management and Lead Tracking Are

What is lead management, and why should you care? Is lead tracking separate from lead management?

What it is: Lead management is the entire, interwoven process of generating, nurturing, and converting leads. Lead tracking is the process of monitoring lead activity and engagement.

Why you should care: Lead management allows businesses to continue to build and develop relationships with potential customers and customers. When practiced skillfully, lead management will provide insights into the effectiveness of the steps prior to lead management (i.e., generation, nurturing, and conversion). A conscientious approach to lead tracking will give a business a "report card" of the lead management processes.

Without lead management and tracking, businesses will not know how effective their strategies are. Often, strategy-setting costs money, and it always involves time. Neither money nor time are resources that a business wants to waste unless they have high hopes of…failing.

What You May Think Lead Management and Lead Tracking Are

We are pretty sure you know what lead management is, and we are pretty sure we agree. However, what we want to emphasize is that lead management is not merely a process. Its importance lies in how the steps of generation, nurturing, and conversion are woven together and that they are revisited as necessary. Lead management may mean that a business revisits a step if lead tracking indicates the step is not impactful. Lead management may mean the business needs to restart or rebuild the relationship if the customer exits the relationship, etc.

At this point, we're confident you know what lead tracking is. Our point of emphasis is that businesses can rely on lead tracking as a compass and a report card as a means to become more efficient with their L2RM strategies.

An In-Depth Look at Lead Management and Tracking

Lead management is a "very active and continuous process" (Strauss, 2023). Effective lead management means that your leads receive information that's going to interest them to the point they are likely to become customers. It's a win-win: your leads don't get annoyed with irrelevant marketing content, and you save time and resources by focusing your efforts on targeted marketing, ultimately increasing profit (Strauss, 2023).

Describing lead management as active, continuous, and "win-win" is spot-on. We especially like the inclusion of the word "continuous" since it is imperative that lead management may involve revisiting, repeating, or reworking certain steps in the process. Despite its overuse ("win-win" is often heard echoing throughout the halls of businesses everywhere), it is an apt description of a desired relationship.

An Example of the Importance of Lead Tracking

Let's go back to Best ERP, Inc., the business that handed out miniature hammers with the tagline, "Contact us to hammer out your next Enterprise Resource Planning (ERP) software solution!" What'Sup Steel interacted with Best ERP, Inc. at the tradeshow, received a miniature hammer, and received the follow-up email inquiring about whether the business's needs were "hammered out yet."

Now, imagine Rosalie is an employee at What'Sup Steel, and she responded to the follow-up email. She sent an email asking about a demo of Best ERP, Inc.'s latest ERP system.

Would it be wise for Best ERP, Inc. to include What'Sup Steel in a list of cold calls that will start happening next week? The purpose of the cold calls is to announce to all iron and steel companies within a 250-mile radius of Best ERP, Inc. that they're releasing their latest ERP system. Without checking their CRM system, Best ERP, Inc. called What'Sup Steel.

Unfortunately, that was a waste of Best ERP Inc.'s time and a waste of Rosalie's time. Also, the cold call to What'Sup Steel gave the impression that Best ERP, Inc. couldn't be bothered to keep track of their prospects, which indicated to What'Sup Steel that Best ERP, Inc. didn't care about potential customers. Rosalie assumed that Best ERP, Inc. will care even less once the sales contract is signed. Rosalie called Best ERP, Inc. and considered leaving a message canceling the demo.

However, let's exit the real world for a moment and time warp back to a day or two prior to Best ERP, Inc. starting their cold calls. Imagine that Best ERP, Inc. reviewed their CRM entries. They saw that What'Sup Steel was approached at the tradeshow, received a CTA, received the follow-up email, and that Rosalie from What'Sup Steel contacted Best ERP, Inc.

After reading about What'Sup Steel in the CRM system, Best ERP, Inc. did not include What'Sup Steel in their cold-calling exercise.

It's still good news, even though we've returned to the real world where Best ERP, Inc. called Rosalie at What'Sup Steel. Rosalie remembered working at a steel company as an intern. She helped the director of marketing with a mailer campaign directed at prospects. Mistakenly, Rosalie sent a mailer to an existing customer, who called the director of marketing and reminded them to double-check their mailing lists. The director of marketing had a stern talk with Rosalie about the importance of CRM.

Rosalie remembered the talk and that she got a second chance to work on the next direct mail project. Rosalie assumed that Best ERP, Inc. had an employee (or an intern) who made a similar mistake. She decided not to cancel the demo from Best ERP, Inc. It might have been a harmless mistake that was not indicative of What'Sup Steel's L2RM practices.

Methods of Lead Tracking

Even the businesses with slick websites brimming with concise content as well as accurate and clickable links lose prospects.

Why?

Small design issues that developers overlook can cause people to become confused, hesitant, or lost. Over time, this adds up to a catastrophic loss of opportunities, prospects, and sales (Aston, 2022). In addition to non-intuitive user interfaces or "design quirks," people interact with web content differently. There isn't a one-size-fits-all approach to navigating a business's online content. As such, we need to pay attention to the data collected and conveyed by these lead-tracking technologies.

In addition to CRM systems, which we have cited frequently, there are two other categories of technology that are beneficial to lead tracking.

1. Marketing Automation Platforms (MAPs)

MAPs automate and optimize marketing activities, such as email marketing, lead scoring, and lead nurturing. According to the Digital Marketing Institute, in an article dated December 22, 2022, 80% of the world's top-performing companies using marketing automation technology for the past three or more years have seen a notable boost in revenue as well as consumer engagement.

Eighty percent? We know we have your attention when it comes to MAPs.

How does a MAP work? We have studied marketing processes performed by humans, so what does marketing look like when it's automated?

MAP in Action

1. A user visits Company U's website. Company U sells circuit boards and uses a MAP as part of their L2RM process.

2. On the Company U website is a downloadable brochure about a circuit board they recently patented called EZ-CB. The user must enter their contact information before downloading the brochure.

3. The user downloads the EZ-CB brochure.

4. The downloading action triggers the MAP to send the contact information and what the contact downloaded to Company U's CRM system.

5. An automatic email is sent to the user (think of the way "out of office" emails are sent in response to inbound emails when the user has an "out of office" status set). Thanks to the capabilities of the MAP, the user's name and company name are prefilled in the automatic email.

6. Based on the MAP's configuration, additional emails are sent to the contact who downloaded the EZ-CB brochure.

A MAP saves a business the time and effort of employees. A MAP does not displace employees, as a human is needed to interpret the data recorded and stored by the MAP.

What does the data tell Company U? Is there interest in EZ-CB? How much interest is there, based on the number of emails sent? How many current customers are downloading the EZ-CB brochure?

If these are your questions, let's move from MAPs to analytics and tracking tools.

2. Analytics and Tracking Tools

Analytics and tracking tools designed for lead tracking focus on online users' behavior while they're interacting with the online content. Page views, number of clicks, and fields that are completed within online forms are some of the data points that are trackable.

Okay, so we know what kind of technology is involved, and the data points it collects. As with a CRM system, the technology is only as useful as what we learn from it. Analytic tools take the data and allow it to explain itself.

An Analogy For Analytics

Imagine you are an anthropologist working on a dig site in some remote part of the world. You discover a tomb buried for centuries. Within the tomb are shards of pottery on which characters are inscribed. You're thrilled with the discovery, but you don't know any more about the indigenous people of the area than you did prior to unearthing the tomb. (Okay, so you know they bury their dead, but it ends there. *National Geographic* isn't likely to do a story on that; well, not a feature story, anyway.) In one corner, you find a fish-shaped stone tablet with the Greek alphabet on one side and characters you recognize from the pottery pieces on the other side. You believe you've discovered a second Rosetta Stone!

This is an analogy to the tracking and analytics technology. As the anthropologist, you are in the role of the tracking software. You're gathering pots with writing on them; this is analogous to data collection done by tracking software. The tracking software/the pots contain the data. The stone tablet you found is in the role of the analytics software. The analytics software/the fish-shaped stone will tell you about the data.

What evaluation techniques exist to help us understand our data?

A/B Testing

A/B testing is comparing two versions of the same subject to see which version is the better one. We're going to look at the analytics and data sciences field to explain more about A/B testing, specifically, we're studying *Harvard Business Review's* article dated June 29, 2017.

Kaiser Fung founded the applied analytics program at Columbia University and is the author of Junk Charts, a blog devoted to the critical examination of data and graphics in the mass media (Gallo, 2017).

Fung gave an example of an A/B test, the subject of which was the size of a "Subscribe" button on a website. The metric is the number of users who click the button. Fung described how the test would be run. The tester would show two sets of users the different versions of the "Subscribe" button (the only difference between the two buttons is the size of the button) and determine which influenced the success metric the most. In this example, Fung's success metric is which button size caused more visitors to click (Gallo, 2017).

Heat Maps

Heat maps are not a test like an A/B test. However, they can tell us quite a bit about our data.

A heat map is a visual representation of the concentrations of a variable. Heat maps measure the density of data in a defined area. Said simply, a heat map is a picture that shows viewers where the action is and how much action is happening.

Envision a solar panel business, SunPrisoner, that runs a terrific website. It has succinct product descriptions, downloadable pamphlets for those that want more detail, user reviews and user ratings, and the pages load quickly even when viewed on a mobile device plagued with a weak Wi-Fi signal.

SunPrisoner uses lead tracking and analytics software. By utilizing the "heat map" functionality, SunPrisoner can see the concentration of users of their windows. SunPrisoner can enter criteria into a filter, such as a SunPrisoner window model number and a U.S. region. Using these criteria, a heat map will be generated that shows which windows they manufacture are used in the specified region of the U.S.

Session Playbacks

Like a heat map, a session playback tells us a lot about our data. Playbacks are a compilation of a user's behavior on a website. A playback shows pages viewed, links clicked, buttons clicked (rage clicks, we're looking at you), and at what point the user stopped using the website.

Best Practices

First, a business needs to look at all the concepts (i.e., lead management, data gathering, lead tracking, data analysis) woven together. Second, a business should react to the information, learn from it, and make data-driven decisions. Decisions made based on data are quantifiable and produce empirical evidence. Third, the data-driven decisions should be folded into a business's total L2RM strategy.

A Last Word

In a perfect world, a business will attract many interested parties who become prospects. The prospects will convert to customers who respond to the business's questions and provide constant, constructive feedback about the products or services it uses or chooses not to use. The customers will expand their use of the business's offerings. Additionally, the interested parties who become disinterested won't hesitate to explain, in courteous detail, why the business's solution didn't fit their needs.

That would be wonderful, like world peace and no more middle-aged weight gain. However, those situations don't exist currently.

Some lead management tools collect the data, which has the ability to tell a story. Some lead tracking tools take the data and put it through tests or create visual representations to tell the stories.

Do you recall Rosalie at WhatSup Steel, Best ERP, Inc., and the mailer campaign mishap? Even with the lead tracking and management technology, when a business fails to study its outputs, technology, and methodology cannot be of any use.

In the previous section, Best Practices, we underlined how it is critical to practice each of the concepts together, as a process, as opposed to stand-alone activities.

What does that translate to individual employees within a business?

For the individual working on lead generation, their perspective shouldn't be "I'm responsible for lead generation. I care about content marketing and our business's social media presence, but my job ends there."

It should be "I'm responsible for lead generation. My focus is on content marketing and our business's social media presence, which helps direct outbound leads to what we have to offer. I am building the base for interested parties to become prospects, which need to be nurtured."

For the individual working with prospects by cultivating a relationship, their focus is lead nurturing. Their perspective shouldn't be, "I just need to work on these contacts who filled out our feedback form after the trade show last month. I'll make a few calls and then hope I have some real leads for the sales reps."

It should be "I will focus on the contacts who completed that form, giving feedback on their experience at the trade show. I think I'll touch base with the lead gen team to see if they have had any previous dealings with these contacts. From that, I can provide the sales reps with a start-to-finish picture."

Please understand; we aren't trying to point fingers or shame anyone who has thought of their role as a standalone one. It helps to see how the individual fits into the bigger picture, the whole process, etc. Now, you see the importance of connectivity.

Chapter Four

Revenue Management

What Revenue Management Is

What is revenue management and why should you care?

What it is: Revenue management is the process of maximizing revenue by optimizing pricing, product availability, and demand.

Why you should care: Revenue management ensures businesses are able to convert leads into revenue. Without this conversion, there is no revenue, without revenue, there are no profits, and without profits, the business fails.

What You May Think Revenue Management Is

Many businesspeople see revenue management as a stand-alone function composed of key activities such as pricing optimization and product availability. The first part of the statement is not true; revenue management is not a standalone function any more than lead generation or lead nurturing are. The second part of the statement is true; revenue management is composed of actions such as pricing optimization, product availability, and demand.

Sometimes, businesses have a revenue management department or a chief revenue officer. Owing to that, revenue management can be perceived as a stand-alone function. It is much less likely for a business to have a "lead generation department" or a "lead nurturing department." As such, it is easier to imagine those functions as processes within a sales department.

An In-Depth Look at Revenue Management

There are two in-depth views regarding revenue management. The first is the view that revenue management is a part of a process woven in with lead generation, lead nurturing, lead management, and lead analytics. The second view is that revenue management is an umbrella function under which other activities fall (e.g., price optimization, product availability, etc.)

Both views are true.

Revenue Management: Part of a Process and an Umbrella Function

At the end of the previous chapter, you might remember our descriptions of misconceptions that may be held by those working in lead generation and lead nurturing. We described them as "misconceptions" because the espoused view was that each of those functions are independent, and that those in the roles didn't need to think about the steps in the L2RM process before or after "their step."

Likewise, a revenue management department or a revenue manager must look beyond their immediate responsibilities (i.e., price analysis, product availability, forecasting demand, and inventory management). They should know about the activities that preceded the functions of revenue management.

Revenue management cannot be carried out effectively in a vacuum. Sure, that is another overused phrase, "cannot be carried out effectively in a vacuum," but it is accurate.

Revenue Management as Part of a Process and an Umbrella Function: An Example

The Most Delicious Fruitcake Company (MDFC) is a small, family-owned business. It is busy year-round, despite their primary selling season being the months of November and December.

The Chief Revenue Officer (CRO) is kept up at night thinking about things. These things are the functions of revenue management. The ingredients must be purchased (pricing analysis). They must be sourced and delivered on a schedule (forecasting). The ingredients are perishable (e.g., the fruit, nuts, and butter), so storing them is time-sensitive. Managing the final product, the fruitcake also requires top-notch inventory management as they are perishable (inventory).

The CRO of MDFC works daily with the tasks usually associated with revenue management (e.g., pricing, forecasting, inventory management). In the CRO's view, the most important job is converting corporate leads to corporate customers, who will rely on MDFC as their fruitcake supplier.

In addition to the tasks associated with traditional revenue management, the CRO and the teams study heat maps to see where in the U.S. and in the world fruitcake is popular (this is no small task because the dessert's popularity has been waning). The CRO works with the marketing department to see how fruitcake might be positioned in other European countries. In Italy, panettone is a dessert similar to fruitcake. Perhaps there is an untapped market there.

As such, the CRO is beyond busy. She doesn't think she needs to understand leads before they become customers. She doesn't see the value in considering revenue management as one part of a process.

We respectfully disagree.

Eunice works within the lead generation group at MDFC. Eunice has noticed a trend with the potential leads that do not progress beyond the prospect stage. At least three contacts have told her that they do not like the traditional British spelling and word choice on the MDFC fruitcake packaging. One contact told Eunice that fruitcake is actually a storied tradition in the southern U.S., and they don't think the fruitcake should be associated uniquely with England.

Would Eunice's information be useful to the CRO? Yes. The heat maps the CRO studies don't tell her about the consumers that don't become consumers. Having insight from Eunice would be useful to the CRO, as she would know the reason that three leads did not convert. For a small business, three corporate leads that didn't convert should be considered relevant data points.

Revenue Management Activities

We've mentioned some of the activities that fall under the revenue management umbrella. We'll get into the specifics.

Pricing Optimization

Pricing optimization is exactly what it sounds like it is. It's setting prices to maximize revenue. Why is that important to revenue management? The price that customers are willing to pay has a direct impact on revenue.

If the price is set too low, the business is losing potential earnings if the prospects are willing to pay more than the set price. If the price is set too high, the business is losing potential earnings because not enough prospects are willing to pay the set price.

The Factors that Affect Pricing Optimization

7 Learnings is a software company based in Germany, focused on the retail sector. In an article published on their website, dated March 15, 2021, there are seven factors that might affect price optimization.

- competition

- weather

- season

- special events/holidays

- macroeconomic variables

- operating costs

- warehousing costs

Take into account that some of these factors are more prevalent in the retail world. Most of the transactions happen between a business and hundreds, if not thousands, of consumers. In business-to-business transactions, there are fewer individual transactions and fewer consumers, but the individual transactions have a much higher price tag.

For a business-to-consumer example, consider an electronics retailer selling smartphones to individuals. For a business-to-business example, consider our Best ERP, Inc. selling an ERP software system to WhatSup Steel.

The Value of Pricing Optimization

The more data that is gathered and the thoroughness with which it is analyzed can be used to affect business decisions. Data (gathered through lead management technology) and analysis (performed by analytics software and assessed by employees) can convey patterns and trends.

An Example of Pricing Optimization

Recall our fruitcake manufacturer, MDFC, and their use of heat maps as a tool to see where fruitcake sales are most plentiful. In January of 2023, MDFC noticed that fruitcake sales in the southeastern U.S. were 12% higher in November and December of 2022 than they were in the same geographic region in November and December of 2021.

Unsure of the reason for that difference (the CRO had not yet realized the importance of talking with the lead generation and nurturing employees), MDFC made plans to increase their advertising budget for the southeastern U.S. starting in the third quarter of 2023.

Their decision was based on a demonstrably higher increase in fruitcake demand in the southeastern U.S. in 2022, and they wanted to stimulate that interest before the buying season in November and December of 2023.

Product Availability Management

Product availability management is the process of making sure the quantity of the product is obtainable according to the demand for the product. Stock availability has been in the headlines of the news with the onset and development of the COVID-19 pandemic.

Check out the following list of stock availability challenges (Severn, 2023).

- supply chain bottlenecks
- unexpected customer orders
- forecast errors
- supplier issues
- missing data

- angry customers

- supplier payment issues

- disrupted processes

Any one of those, not to mention a combination, can throw even the most seasoned revenue manager into a string of sleepless nights. Supply chain bottlenecks might mean that the printed circuit boards you're manufacturing can't be made until your suppliers of copper and fiberglass resolve their transportation problems.

What can one do about product availability and the issues that plague it?

Option One: Prioritization

One possible solution is to prioritize.

"It's all important! I can't pick one customer over another when it comes to product availability!" we hear you saying. Yes, it is all-important, we hear you and sympathize. However, it is about prioritizing based on timing and urgency, not prioritizing based on importance.

Some product availability issues have a bigger impact in terms of the time requirements and urgency. This is especially tricky in the services industry.

A business has two customers, and each of them spends about $1.5 million dollars per year on your business's services.

Two weeks ago, Business A signed a three-year contract with your company. The contract is worth $4.5 million dollars. They are counting on your business to send a consulting team onsite starting in one week.

Multi-year customer, Business B, is expecting a consulting team onsite to correct an error made by a previous consulting team from your company. The new team is set to start on the same date as Business A. Due to an allocation error, the same consulting team is booked for Business A and Business B.

What do you do? Which business, A or B, is more important? That shouldn't be the question. The question should be, "Which business has a more urgent need? Which business will be most impacted by timing?"

In order to make those determinations, other factors should be included. Think about these as possible questions to ask:

1. What is the impact of the mistake that your business's team made with Business B?

2. For Business B, is it a financial or a legal impact, or is it both?

3. Will the mistake made by the prior team with Business B result in a negative impact on Business B's customers?

4. What kind of timing is required to rectify the mistakes for Business B?

5. What is driving the consultant team's start date for Business A?

6. Does Business A require in-depth subject matter knowledge from your business's consulting team?

Option Two: Designated Teams and Automation

Another possible solution is two-part. The first part is having entry-level employees or those who are new to the field (whether it's sales, marketing, pricing, or supply chain) assigned to a set of straightforward tasks. The second part is to automate the tasks that can be turned over to a computer or a machine.

Designated Teams

What is the best way to learn about a field in which you are new? Learning by doing is the prevailing wisdom. We agree.

When you first imagined your sales career, you might have thought in terms of multi-million dollar deals and jetting between cities in which your top clients are headquartered. Those are two aspects of some types of sales, but not all, and definitely not when one is starting out.

To be assigned to multi-million dollar deals or top clients, one must know their employer's products and services, like one knows their name, address, and telephone number. How have your business's services evolved, or what game-changing features were added to your business's products? Who uses your products, and what are their existing concerns? One must also know the industry in which their employer operates and who the competition is. What are the significant ways in which your employer's offerings differ from the competitors? Can you cite publicly available success stories and statistics for your employer's products and services?

The only way one acquires this knowledge is through living the experiences of cold calling, studying heat maps, comparing sales funnels, reviewing user data, and talking with potential leads. Having new or reallocated employees dedicated to these types of activities is beneficial for teaching purposes. It's also beneficial to the company if the activities can be distributed to those who can learn from them and distributed away from those whose focus needs to be elsewhere.

A newly minted college graduate may have worked with the latest and greatest order management software. They can recite the top ten innovations in sales technology in the last 18 months. They can quote case studies. They created a brilliant A/B testing model for their senior project.

A newly-minted college graduate won't know a single thing about the business's warm leads that are transitioning to hot leads. They don't know the current topics being discussed at tradeshows and industry events. They don't know the reasons the business's cold leads failed to convert to warm leads. They don't know the time frames between follow-ups with the company's top three prospects. They don't know which customers have been long-term customers, and they don't know why they have the tenure they do.

The college graduates (as well as those who are transitioning to a new role or coming from another industry) are perfectly suited to pick up the straightforward and rote tasks. They can learn about the business from cold calling, studying web analytics data, following up with warm prospects, etc. The more seasoned pricing analysts, business development managers, and sales reps can spend less time on those types of tasks and more time in their specialized roles.

Automation

In today's business world, we are permeated with technology. It is easy to assume that whatever machine-based shortcuts exist, they're already in place. Surprisingly, many businesses are discovering time-saving solutions, and some boast a bevy of other benefits.

To underline the "wow" factor of automation's advancement, we'll go outside of L2RM. Check out one of *Time*'s most notable inventions of 2022: Vicarious Surgicals system puts a virtual reality (VR) headset and operable robot limbs into the hands of surgeons. Surgeons use these devices with patients in the operating room! The goal is to make surgeries safer, as the system allows a much smaller incision on the human body. According to Vicarious Surgical CEO Adama Sachs, "Complication rates from open surgeries are 15% to 20%, just from the incision...by making incisions really small ... you can knock complication rates down to about 1%." (Alderton, 2022).

In the realm of L2RM, for a technological system designed to deal with product availability issues, we'll take a look at retail giant: Walmart.

Fresh From the Field: Product Availability Automation at Work at Walmart ("Walmart Sets the Standard with Supply Chain Automation," 2023).

For Walmart, having the right products in the right place at the right time is no small feat.

"With 10,000 stores and 2.2 million employees across 24 countries, Walmart is looking to leverage new frontiers in an automated supply chain to reduce costs, fulfill orders more efficiently, and improve the customer experience." ("Walmart Sets the Standard with Supply Chain Automation." 2023, paragraph 1).

To make this goal a reality, Walmart established its Walmart Global Tech group, which estimates that by 2026, more than two-thirds of their stores will have some type of automation.

While you've used Walmart's website to order online or ordered through their app, Walmart is gathering information about your interactions with their site or app, what you purchase, and the quantities of items you purchase. Walmart is using that information to develop artificial intelligence (AI) that will predict customer buying patterns. The goal is to ensure Walmart has the right mix and quantity of products available when their customers want to buy them.

If that is too Big Brother for your taste, know that this kind of data collection predates the internet and phone apps. Retail loyalty cards (e.g., a food retailer issues plastic cards imprinted with a barcode to shoppers that they swipe each time they shop in exchange for future discounts on items) perform the same function.

In their stores, employees who work for Walmart have or will have handheld devices. The devices receive real-time information that is conveyed electronically about product inventory and prices.

Think of the time that is saved for both the employee and the customer. If a customer does not see the brand and type of shampoo they want, they ask an employee. Before automation, the employee had to go into the storage area, look for the area in which shampoo is stored, look for the brand and type needed by the customer, and return to the customer to share the information. While the employee was away, the customer may have decided to go to another store or buy another kind of shampoo. Both of those data points (pieces of market intelligence) would be unnoticed and unrecorded because the employee was searching the storage shelves for shampoo.

Moving from the retail store to the fulfillment center, let's see how automation works behind the scenes, but still within the Walmart organization. Manufacturers and suppliers send their products to Walmart, and Walmart sells them. The fulfillment center is where the products arrive and fall into the hands of robots. This isn't an episode of *Battlestar Galactica*; this is reality. A robot in a Walmart fulfillment center receives stores, and retrieves products.

Moving from the fulfillment center to the interactions between Walmart and its suppliers, we still see automation at work. Walmart's data flows via a system called Real Link. Real Link conveys information to the suppliers, who use it to forecast demand and plan inventory. If the suppliers know what products are frequently bought and the number of units of each product that are purchased, they will ensure Walmart has what it needs so Walmart's customers get what they need.

Concerns regarding employee reduction often surface in the face of automation. For certain jobs, the need for employees will be reduced. However, that does not mean the need for employees will decrease as a whole. Employees that may have packed crates, unloaded pallets, and searched for stock on foot can be retrained. With automation, thousands of jobs are anticipated to be created in the work areas of quality control, process auditing, and flow management. Those who currently work in those areas will have valuable skills and knowledge to transfer to the incoming employees through training programs and workshops.

Other benefits to employees include a safer work environment (on the presumption that the robots make fewer mistakes than humans) and a decrease in the physical demands of some jobs. With less physical rigor and less risk involved in some jobs, there may be more opportunities for people with disabilities or people who are aging. This may lead to a shift in the current employee population, diversifying and enriching the current workforce.

Demand Management

Demand management is the mirror image of product availability but on the business-impacting side rather than the customer-impacting side. Think of looking in the mirror.

If you wave at yourself with your right hand, your reflection is waving with its left hand. When the desired products are available to the customer when and where they want them, that indicates the business's demand management is optimized. When the business's inventory is arriving and departing from the fulfillment center, it is available in the retail stores in conjunction with when customers want it, which indicates the business knows what the level of product availability should be.

Demand management can be very difficult to optimize. Customer needs fluctuate based on seasonality, personal taste, trends, and timing. Thus, mastering demand management truly is trying to hit a moving target.

The likelihood of hitting the target is increased with lead management and tracking. By amassing data, identifying patterns, and spotting trends, demand management can be easier to execute.

Consider the changes that have happened in the healthcare industry due to COVID-19. The top five trends in healthcare for 2023 are AI as it affects healthcare, remote healthcare offerings, retail healthcare, wearable medical devices, and personalized healthcare (Marr, 2022). If your business is in the technology sector, even if it is unrelated to clinical medicine, you may want to focus on what type of technology might be applicable to the medical community. Imagine you are at the helm of your business, and your business produces software for materials resource planning (MRP). Considering the things that may be in demand, you are considering your MRP software in light of the top five healthcare trends.

Wearable medical devices need to be manufactured; they are not a service and therefore require physical materials in order to be made. Thinking strategically, you might advise your marketing and business development teams to begin researching medical device providers. Medical device providers may be seeing a sharp increase due to people who require wearable medical devices. Thus, medical device providers may be potential customers for your business's MRP software as they scramble to have the pieces and parts available to meet customer demands.

Tying the Three Revenue Management Activities Together

Revenue management is the final link in the L2RM chain, relying on the previous links (e.g., lead generation, lead conversion, etc.) to create an unbreakable chain. Within revenue management are key activities. These are pricing optimization, product availability, and demand management, the pillars of successful revenue management.

So, how do you know it's working?

What, you're thinking, *what do you mean*?

We've reviewed these concepts. We understand how they matter and why they matter, and have studied real-life examples in which these concepts unfold.

How does a business know the L2RM chain is strong? How can a business tell if their pricing optimization, product availability, and demand management are doing what they're supposed to do, i.e., supporting a top-notch revenue management link?

You're thinking, *we covered this*; *we record the data and analyze it to inform us whether our L2RM practices are thriving*.

Okay, the data is recorded, and now it can be analyzed. Who records it? Who analyzes it?

If you're recalling what we briefly covered in Chapter Three, technology and its ability to track and analyze data points (e.g., mouse clicks within a page), you're right. Chapter Three introduced the technology and some of the ways it is put to use to determine if your L2RM practices are working.

Next up, we'll get a bit more detailed regarding the data points the technologies collect and how the data points are analyzed.

Tools and Technologies That Support Revenue Management

There are three categories of technology tools that measure different aspects of L2RM results. All of the technology tools addressed herein are operating systems or web-based services, or mobile applications.

1. Revenue Management Systems (RMS)

The goal of an RMS is to collect data, identify patterns observed in the data, then construct models or simulations of customer behavior in order to optimize resources and maximize profitability.

Does that sound like more business blather with nothing actionable behind it? We hope not because we think that the definition of an RMS is pretty solid. We'll walk you through it. Examples always help!

An RMS Example

Let's designate our business as a social media platform, JustMyLife. JustMyLife wants to know how many users invite their contacts to join them through the JustMyLife platform during a one-week period. Within the JustMyLife app is an "Invite" button that, when tapped, the app scans the contacts stored in the device on which JustMyLife exists and sends a text message to the contact.

JustMyLife runs an RMS on their servers that are configured with a rule that every time a user's "Invite" button is tapped, the instance is recorded in the user's profile. Also within the RMS is a function to view multiple data points, such as the number of contacts invited by tapping the "Invite" button and the number of times that the "Invite" button was tapped.

"**The goal of RMS is to collect data**." JustMyLife's RMS is performing that function. It counts taps per user, contacts invited, and the number of times the "Invite" button was tapped.

"The goal of RMS is to collect data, **identify patterns observed in the data**..." The business analysts at JustMyLife have been trained on the specific functionalities and capabilities of the RMS. Once they complete training, they're called "power users." The power users know how to run queries, create heat maps, and overlay different data points to generate reports that showcase one or more user behaviors. The power users compile the queries, heat maps, and user behavior tracking.

"The goal of RMS is to collect data, identify patterns observed in the data, and **then construct models or simulations of customer behavior**..." With the compilation of queries, heat maps, and user behavior tracking, the power users run different queries to learn that 56% of the registered JustMyLife users clicked the "Invite" button. The RMS has a module within it that calculates there are an average of 125 contacts reached with each tap. The power users are able to see the times of day or night that the "Invite" button was tapped, thanks to the RMS's tracking capability that scans each user profile. The power users build a model, using the RMS's rules and algorithms, to predict how many JustMyLife users will click the "Invite" button if they extend their study by another week.

"The goal of an RMS is to collect data, identify patterns observed in the data, then construct models or simulations of customer behavior **in order to optimize resources and maximize profitability**." The power users put together a deck for the senior management committee, including a summary of what the data tells them about user behaviors and a recommendation to continue the study for another week based on their findings. They discovered that more users were clicking the "Invite" button as the days passed. The senior management committee decides to add more buttons within the app, so their RMS is pulling double duty by providing market intelligence.

2. Data Analytics and Reporting Tools

Data analytics and reporting tools allow businesses to analyze and visualize data from lead management and tracking, as well as identify patterns and trends. These tools sound very similar to RMS, but they are not the same.

Systems described as an RMS focus on specific areas of revenue management, e.g., pricing optimization, availability, and demand forecasting. An RMS is configured with rules, formulae, and algorithms that support those specific areas.

Data analytics and reporting tools are highly useful for revenue management. They are task-focused in nature and have broad applications.

The tasks performed by these tools include data scraping (gathering specific and vast quantities of information from the internet), performing mathematical operations on large sets of data, statistical analysis, data mining, predictive modeling, and data visualization/graphing.

This type of tool is often in the form of software or a web application.

Data analytics and reporting tools can be used to tell the number of orders for a product that are processed each month. By identifying the product by its stock keeping unit (SKU), the SKU is trackable throughout a period of time. A business could use this information to forecast demand for the product. Correctly forecasting demand helps to ensure the products are available when customers want them.

A data analytics and reporting tool can be used to see how many users are accessing a business's website and at what times. This information is necessary in order to create a predictive model. How is a predictive module useful? A business tracking this type of user activity learns what time periods show the least amount of traffic and what the best time is to take the system down for maintenance. No one in their right mind would take a trade order management system offline at 10 a.m. on a Tuesday morning (unless it involved disabling the collateralized debt obligation functionality in 2007). After the major markets close would be the common-sense choice, however, a predictive model would indicate when the fewest number of users are accessing the trade order management system.

3. Business Intelligence Tools

The only thing more valuable than information (about one's customers, one's competitors, etc.) is what you can do with it. A business can hire the most intelligent software engineers and system designers they can afford. These professionals can write code in multiple languages and develop the most thorough data scraping tool in existence. However, if the data can't be presented in a readable, relevant, and user-friendly way, it has no value.

Data, Business Intelligence, and the United Nations (U.N.)

Imagine a meeting is to be held at the U.N. The goal is to brainstorm peace-keeping methods for a country with two warring indigenous groups, E and F.

The meeting attendees comprise representatives from the indigenous groups and six consultants. The six consultants come from a variety of fields. Two were embedded in war-torn nations and assisted the governments in setting up a code of laws. Two worked for political parties within countries that were establishing their first democratic government after centuries of dictator rule. Two served with various peace-keeping agencies. All six consultants speak English and French. Neither the people of group E nor the people of group F understand English or French. None of the six consultants speak the languages of Group E or Group F.

While the six consultants bring years of knowledge and subject matter expertise, they cannot convey it in a way that indigenous groups E and F understand. Data that is not easily presented and understood is the equivalent of the six consultants. If the six consultants had an interpreter (it is the U.N., and one should be lurking in the halls somewhere), they would be infinitely valuable. Business intelligence is the equivalent of an interpreter. Operations of every type are performed on the data, but it won't "say" anything without business intelligence, which conveys actionable information.

Key Performance Indicators (KPIs)

KPIs are a business's version of the grades that students earn at school. To keep it simple, think back to your early years of education. Math, reading, spelling, science, and social studies were the subjects you might have studied under the tutelage of an instructor. Periodically, the instructor would test the students to determine how well they were learning the subject matter. Every so many weeks or months, a cumulative score was assigned for each subject based on how you performed on exams, tests, and homework.

KPIs refer to a set of countable metrics used to gauge a company's overall long-term performance. KPIs are the checkpoints that focus on a company's strategic, budgetary, and operational benchmarks. The checkpoints should be commensurate with the checkpoints that are evaluated by other businesses that serve the same markets (Twin, 2023).

KPIs vary depending on the type of business. An investment management firm might have KPIs focused on aspects of investment portfolio performance in a specific sector. A manufacturing company might have KPIs for efficiency, adherence to product specifications, and the number of days since the last safety incident. A retailer might have KPIs for customer satisfaction ratings based on numerical scores. Surely you've completed a customer feedback form online or a paper-based one at some point. A scorecard might be presented to a customer with this kind of message: "On a scale of one to five, with one being 'terrible' and five being 'best.' Please rate these aspects of our hotel; cleanliness, friendliness of front desk staff, efficiency when checking in, dining options, available amenities, efficiency when checking out."

There are four types of KPIs (Twin, 2023).

- Strategic KPIs are measurements of big-picture goals. By how much did the total revenue earned in the calendar year of 2021 exceed the total revenue earned in the calendar year 2020? Did the number of new clients exceed a growth of 5%?

- Functional KPIs measure individual department goals. How many smart templates did the software engineering team create in Q2 vs. Q1? How many customer accounts were added by the strategic sales team in Q4?

- Operational KPIs measure the performance of discrete functions over a period of time. A gourmet cookie bakery sold a decreasing quantity of chocolate chip cookies in the months of October, November, and December, while the number of cinnamon swirl cookies sold in the same months changed by less than 1%. These KPIs (chocolate chip cookie sales and cinnamon swirl cookie sales for the months of October, November, and December) might be examined in light of the bakery changing from one butter supplier to another, but only for the butter used in the chocolate chip cookies.

- Leading or lagging KPIs indicate a trend for a type of data to ascertain what may happen in the future or what might have happened in the past that created a certain circumstance. The gourmet cookie bakery decreased the number of bakers working in October, November, and December but did not adjust cookie output. The decrease in the baker workforce may be a leading KPI that indicates that fewer bakers working create less-desirable cookies. The gourmet cookie bakery increased the types of cookies they will sell in January, February, and March. A lagging KPI might indicate that fewer chocolate chip and cinnamon swirl cookies will be sold based on a broader selection from which customers choose.

By studying KPIs, a business can build its knowledge and understanding of their customers. It's another way data points can be conveyed, and trends can be identified. Through that step, a business can develop business intelligence that will drive revenue management strategy.

A Whirlwind Tour Through Tools and Technology

Revenue management systems, data analytics and reporting tools, and business intelligence applications can do wonders for gathering vital data as well as configuring it in a way that tells a story. In the next chapter, we'll get deeper into the bits and bytes when it comes to understanding what makes these technologies useful.

A Last Word

It's funny for a book about revenue management to introduce revenue management as a topic in a later chapter. We think you know why the topic of revenue management becomes front and center at this point in the book.

If you're saying, "L2RM is an intertwined process in which revenue management links to lead identification, lead generation, lead nurturing, lead conversion, data gathering, and data analysis." Thus, it makes total sense that we introduced the process link by link. As revenue management is the last link, it appears in a later chapter.

Next up is an in-depth look at how we can measure L2RM performance and learn how to optimize it.

Chapter Five

Measuring and Optimizing Performance

Whether we have an appreciation or love for numbers, they are a necessity for any kind of objective assessment when it comes to gauging the success of your L2RM processes. Without a standard of quantitative metrics or empirical evidence, many assessments become a series of "I think" statements.

Imagine standing in front of the members of your company's C-suite, and the vice president of operations asks you about the impacts of the new CRM system. Add to that situation the fact that you're the one who led the research, investigation, and evaluation of CRM providers. Your team authored the RFP, led the question and answer sessions with bidders, analyzed the bid packages, and ultimately chose the CRM provider. The CRM system cost half a million dollars, including the software, installation, and consultation. (It also cost you a getaway weekend with friends, five of your children's soccer games, and your mother-in-law's birthday brunch. The only things you gained during the process were six pounds, a prescription antacid, and many late nights in the office.)

Would you answer the question by saying, "The new CRM system is great! We really like it and think you should, too."

If you have any hope of keeping your job after you exit the C-suite (or are escorted out), we implore you not to give that kind of answer.

That said, we are sympathetic and understanding of the complicated nature of the question. The various vice presidents do not want an adjective-packed narrative for each step of the bid process, nor do they want to know the formulae your tech wizards wrote as part of the rules library. We are assuming that the vice presidents are like many business leaders and want to know if the money and efforts spent on the new CRM system have met or exceeded the quantitative expectations they had for the system…in as few words as possible.

What It Means to Measure and Optimize Performance

When you're done cringing at the fictional situation described, you know the answer to a question regarding the impact of a system or set of processes must be provable. One significant way to demonstrate proof is by establishing variables that can be tracked and measured.

The Value of Measurements

Caroline is training to run a mile as fast as she can. Her friend, Kendall, told Caroline she wants to see Caroline decrease her mile time over the course of six weeks.

Caroline writes a training plan. Before she begins the training plan, Caroline runs for one mile on the first day of the six weeks. It takes her five minutes and forty seconds to run one mile.

Over the next six weeks, she commits to each run, regardless of the weather or her job. She records each distance she runs and the time that it takes her to run the distance.

After two weeks, Caroline runs for one mile. It takes her five minutes and thirty-eight seconds. She has dropped by two seconds. After four weeks, Caroline runs for one mile. It takes her five minutes and thirty-two seconds. After six weeks, Caroline runs for one mile. It takes her five minutes and twenty-nine seconds.

Completing each workout is important, and testing her ability to run a mile throughout her training is also important. However, Caroline would not be able to tell how much she improved (or didn't) if she didn't record each mile time she ran. Thus, when she tells Kendall she dropped eleven seconds, she can prove it.

That is what we mean when we say, "L2RM processes and systems, as well as their outputs, must be measurable." The next step after measuring performance is to improve it through optimization.

The Value of Optimization

Optimization is making the most efficient use of the resources you have. "Efficient" means that money, time, and supplies are maximized. At its simplest, optimization can be exemplified through cups and a bucket.

Your responsibility is to remove all the water from the bathtub. Assume it does not have a drain. You have two options. You can use a four-ounce paper cup or a five-gallon bucket. Which would you choose? The five-gallon bucket is the optimal choice. If you chose the four-ounce paper cup, you would waste the energy and exertion it takes to bend and scoop water into the cup. You would waste a lot of time. If you chose the five-gallon bucket, you would be able to collect more water with each scooping movement, and it would take less time. As it would take less time and effort to use the five-gallon bucket, it is the optimal choice.

That is why we say that "L2RM processes and systems, as well as their outputs, must be measurable *and optimized*."

Measuring L2RM Processes and Systems

Measuring L2RM processes and systems begins with lead generation and ends with revenue growth. Here we go with the "links in a chain" metaphor that you know so well. A business does not start measuring the success or failure of an aspect of L2RM in the revenue growth stage.

Imagine the discussion if that were the case. Two revenue managers are trying to determine their L2RM success in 2021 and in 2022. They're looking at a snapshot of revenue growth at the end of the fourth quarter for the respective years.

The snapshot shows that in the last month of the fourth quarter of 2021, the company revenue was X. In 2022, the company revenue was X + 2%. Would either revenue manager conclude that 2022 was more successful because of their L2RM processes and systems?

We doubt they would draw that conclusion.

Our doubts exist because:

1. The revenue managers were looking at two numbers only to gauge the success of L2RM, which were the revenue in 2021 and in 2022.

2. Revenue growth is only one chain in L2RM, and without viewing other variables or gaining context, there is no way to tell how or why revenue increased by 2%.

What is an improved way of evaluating the success of their L2RM processes and systems?

Measuring Lead Generation

The revenue managers need to look back in time to the lead generation phases for 2021 and 2022.

A set of data points they might consider are the transitions from cold to warm to hot leads by the number of prospects as they progressed or did not progress within a set period of time. Another data point might be how many prospects failed to progress to the next level of lead on a quarterly basis.

Measuring Lead Nurturing

Through the insights of their respective teams, the revenue managers might want to study the methods used for lead nurturing.

Based on the target market, was the right mix of personalization, calls-to-action, and lead magnets utilized? Their teams will need to identify how many sales activities used each type of nurturing and note whether there were fluctuations from quarter to quarter.

Measuring Lead Conversion

By studying the leads that were converted, the revenue management teams might want to survey the new customers, asking for their reasons they chose to buy or procure the products or services.

By observing their answers, the teams will be able to tell if new customers' reasons were "clustered." In other words, did multiple new customers cite the same specific reasons, such as "improved product offerings" and "products available when I wanted them?"

Measuring Revenue Growth

We purposefully started by looking only at revenue growth. From that point, we progressed in reverse (don't think too hard about that suggestion as it sounds like we're borrowing from George Lucas's non-linear timelines again!) through the phases of L2RM leading up to revenue growth. The critical thing to remember is that one must have selected metrics to be monitored, then one must record them. If one doesn't record the metrics, no one will be able to tell progress.

Optimizing L2RM Processes and Systems

We'll keep to our example with the two revenue managers who are comparing 2021 and 2022 in terms of revenue growth. We've decided that they need to look at all the links in the L2RM chain, and they need to decide which variables they will monitor and measure. We'd suggest that they do the same exercise with lead optimization.

Optimizing Lead Generation

To measure lead generation, we opined that the two revenue managers would be wise to measure the transitions from cold to warm to hot leads by the number of prospects as they progressed or did not progress within a set period of time. They could measure the number of prospects that failed to progress to the next level of lead on a quarterly basis.

Lead Generation Data Collection

Assume the revenue managers' teams tracked the transition from cold leads to warm leads for January, February, and March of 2021 and the same months in 2022.

In January 2021, three cold leads became warm leads. In February of 2021, two cold leads became warm leads. In March of 2021, one cold lead became a warm lead.

In January 2022, four cold leads became warm leads. In February of 2022, three cold leads became warm leads. In March of 2022, three cold leads became warm leads.

It was obvious that in the first quarter of 2021, fewer leads were generated each month that also converted from cold to warm. In the first quarter of 2022, a greater number of leads were generated each month that also converted from cold to warm.

<u>Lead Generation Data Analysis</u>

The team analysts were pedantic (and correctly so) when they stated that when compared to the first quarter of 2022, not only were there fewer leads from month to month in the first quarter of 2021, but the number of leads that converted from cold to warm in the first quarter of 2021 also decreased.

From an optimization perspective, what would you do if you were one of the revenue managers?

It might be a good idea to look at the environment and variables in the first quarters of 2021 and 2022.

1. Were businesses rebounding from COVID-19 in 2021 and not seeking new solutions yet? Were the same businesses much stronger in 2022 and seeking new solutions?

2. What conferences and industry events were taking place in 2021 and 2022?

3. Were the employees on the sales teams the same in 2021 and 2022?

4. Did the marketing and public relations outreaches change from 2021 to 2022?

5. Should the revenue manager ask themself the same questions 1–4, but for the fourth quarters of 2020 and 2021? "Why would they do that?" you may ask yourself. If you answered yourself, "Perhaps the catalysts occurred prior to the quarter in which the results were analyzed," you'd be correct!

<u>Lead Generation Optimization</u>

Let's focus on one aspect only. The business analysts recognized that a global industry event occurred in January of 2022 and promoted the importance of the particular type of software solution sold by the business. The global industry event did not occur in January 2021 because COVID-19 protocols were still in place.

From an optimization perspective, the revenue manager might encourage the business to promote their software suite in conjunction with the global industry event in 2023. Assuming the business is drawing a conclusion that the global industry event was the catalyst that drove lead generation to a higher level in 2022, the business may want to be proactive in 2023. Maybe they assign their more experienced salespersons to conduct lead generation in conjunction with the global industry event. That's optimization.

Optimizing Lead Nurturing

To optimize lead nurturing, a business should identify measurable behavior demonstrated by the warm leads as they transitioned or didn't transition to hot leads within a set period of time. The revenue managers could measure the quantity of prospects that failed to progress to the next level of lead on a quarterly basis.

Lead Nurturing Data Collection

Assume the revenue managers' teams tracked the transition from warm leads to hot leads for April, May, and June of 2021 and the same months in 2022.

In April 2021, one warm lead became a hot lead.

In April 2022, three warm leads became hot leads.

The team analysts stated that in the first month of the second quarter of 2021, there was one warm lead that became a hot lead. In the first month of the second quarter in 2022, there were three warm leads that converted to hot leads.

Lead Nurturing Data Analysis

From an optimization perspective, what would you do if you were one of the revenue managers?

It might be a good idea to look at the environment and variables in the first month of the second quarter for both 2021 and 2022.

1. How frequently did the sales team follow up with the warm leads in 2021 and in 2022?

2. What types of follow-up did they use?

3. Were the sales representatives that followed up with the warm leads more or less experienced in 2022 than in 2021?

Lead Nurturing Optimization

Let's focus on one aspect only. The business analysts checked the number of times the sales representatives followed up in 2021 and 2022. Since the business is emphatic about using CRM, the contact details were logged in 2021 and 2022.

In 2021, the follow-ups were done electronically. For a period of three weeks after the lead was categorized as "warm," the sales representatives sent one email per week to the contact person. In 2022, the follow-ups were done through phone calls. For a period of three weeks after the lead was categorized as "warm," the sales representatives telephoned the contacts once per week, timing their telephone calls to mid-week and mid-morning.

From an optimization perspective, the revenue manager might assume that the voice-to-voice contact was more effective than the one-way electronic contact for warm leads during a time period of approximately one month. The assumption is based on one warm lead that converted to a hot lead in 2021 and three warm leads that converted to three hot leads in 2022. Maybe, for warm leads identified in 2023, the revenue manager insists that for the month immediately following, contact with the prospects be via telephone.

Optimizing Lead Conversion

To measure lead conversion, a business should identify measurable behavior demonstrated by the hot leads as they transitioned or didn't transition to paying customers. The revenue managers could measure the number of hot leads that failed to progress to paying customers.

Lead Conversion Data Collection

Assume the revenue managers' teams tracked the transition from hot leads to paying customers in the month of May of 2021 and May of 2022.

In May 2021, one hot lead became a paying customer.

In May 2022, two hot leads became paying customers.

The team analysts stated that in the second month of the second quarter of 2021, there was one hot lead that became a customer. In the second month of the second quarter in 2022, there were two hot leads that converted to customers.

Lead Conversion Data Analysis

The team analysts recognized that 100% of the hot leads in May 2021 became paying customers; however, there was only one. The team analysts pointed out that only 66% of the hot leads in May 2022 became paying customers, but unlike in May 2021, there was more than one hot lead.

From an optimization perspective, what would you do if you were one of the revenue managers?

It might be a good idea to look at the environment and variables in the second month of the second quarter for both 2021 and 2022.

1. In 2021, 100% of the hot leads signed sales agreements. As that was only one hot lead that converted to being a customer, should we study the environment and variables in the months prior to May in order to get a full picture?

2. In 2022, why did one of the three hot leads fail to convert to a customer?

Lead Conversion Optimization

Let's focus on one aspect only. Would it be sensible for the revenue manager to focus on the cause behind one hot lead transitioning to a customer in 2021 and two transitioning to customers in 2022?

It's always a good idea to know what made a prospect decline to sign a sales agreement. However, in this situation, with a very small quantity of hot leads in both years, it is a better idea to focus on what led to the minimal hot leads.

A revenue manager that asks a different type of question based on the situation having a very small number of data points is using great judgment. Rather than proceeding with the same type of assessment as they have in previous years, they recognized a different approach is needed.

Optimizing Revenue Growth

Let's go back to the start of the conversation about measuring revenue growth. In the last month of the fourth quarter of 2021, the company revenue was X. In the last month of the fourth quarter of 2022, the company revenue was X + 2%. It's pretty straightforward that the revenue grew by 2% in 2022.

However, our revenue managers are wiser now that they've evaluated the links in the chain prior to the formation of the final link (revenue growth).

Data Collection to Ascertain Revenue Growth

The revenue managers know to instruct their teams to collect data points across multiple months in the lead generation phase, the lead nurturing phase, and the lead conversion phase. They also advise their teams to pay attention to the time frames in which the data points were gathered.

Data Analysis of Revenue Growth

The business analysts consider the potential catalysts and the variables.

1. In the lead generation phase, what was similar and different in the world in the first quarter of 2021 and 2022? Within their industry, what events were taking place?

2. In the lead nurturing phase, what methods were used to reach out to those prospects who progressed to be warm leads?

3. In the lead conversion phase, what valuable information is available, despite the very small number of hot leads becoming paying customers?

4. During what phase or transition did the greatest change occur?

Revenue Growth Optimization

The revenue managers and their teams decide to reevaluate each of the three phases. They noticed the most fluctuation occurred during the lead generation phase in both years.

Recall that in the first quarter of 2021, there were three cold leads in January, and by March, only one had converted to a warm lead. Recall that in the first quarter of 2022, there were four cold leads in January, and by March, three had converted to warm leads.

The sales and analyst teams decide to go through the CRM logs for the first quarter of each 2021 and 2022. They plan to cross-reference follow-up activities with cold leads progressing or not progressing.

Armed with CRM data juxtaposed with lead activity (i.e., which cold leads became warm leads, which cold leads chose not to go forward), the teams are going to overlay their knowledge of the global and industry events.

With those three data types (e.g., CRM data, lead activity, global and industry events), the teams will learn the source of fluctuation in the lead generation phase.

A Last Word on Measuring and Optimizing

As demonstrated, there are many variables and catalysts at work in the world and within industries. Looking at these data points in context with lead tracking and management will help businesses identify the weak and strong links in the L2RM processes and systems.

Thanks to thorough definitions and examples, we are pretty certain you grasp the importance of measuring and optimizing. In the next section, we are going to study the types of metrics a business can use to evaluate the effectiveness of their L2RM process.

Key Metrics

There are several key metrics that businesses can use to track and measure their L2RM performance and effectiveness.

KPIs are the formal gowns of the business world. Formal gowns come in an array of styles that include a sheath, empire waist, princess cut, strapless, and backless. Just as every figure is unique, the formal gown they choose will be, too. Every business (like every formal gown-wearer) has its own defined set of strategies, target customers, and processes. Each business must assess their structure and function to figure out the right metrics.

We agree!

Snigdha Patel of REVEChat identified three considerations that will define a business's KPIs and determine what metrics to track. Patel noted:

1. Who is your target audience?

2. Does your target audience comprise business-to-consumer customers (B2C) or business-to-business customers (B2B)?

3. What is the pricing model? Is your business selling services or products? What is the average dollar value of each transaction (B2C) or deal (B2B)? Are there discrete variables within the pricing model that have the greatest impact on the overall cost?

Please understand that there are differences among the variables within metrics based on the business and industry. For example, Company 115 might define lead initiation type differently than Company 116. Metrics like revenue per lead and customer lifetime value may be calculated differently as well. It's vital to understand the methods used by the company that employs you.

Lead Generation Metrics

Lead generation metrics focus on measuring leads in the critical first phase of business-to-prospect interaction. Aspects like lead volume and lead interaction are helpful. They're straightforward to grasp.

Lead Volume

Lead volume is the number of leads that exist. If a business wants to be able to track lead volume as a metric, they need to know the time period in which the leads are generated. Otherwise, lead volume is a number that says nothing.

Consider the following situation:

"The first quarter lead volume is great! We had 40 cold leads as of January 1 and as of March 29, there are 25 warm leads," said Sales Representative One.

"The new lead volume is better! We had 50 cold leads, and now 47 of them are warm leads," said Sales Representative Two.

If Sales Representative Two is referring to the second quarter of the same year as Sales Representative One, April through the end of June, their statement makes sense, based on comparing two identical time periods (though more data points for both periods are needed to make the statement more credible).

Just to keep it interesting, another way of measuring the success of lead generation is by studying the types of lead initiations chosen that move a lead from one phase to the next phase.

Lead Initiation Type

"Type of lead initiation" refers to how the lead came to be a lead. Were potential leads contacted by a telephone call, an email, interaction at an industry event, etc.?

For Service M, six potential leads were contacted by telephone, and four of the six indicated they were interested. Also, for Service M, thirty potential leads received a promotional email, and ten of the thirty indicated they were interested. Finally, for Service M, four potential leads were approached by Service M sales reps at a conference, and three of the potential leads indicated they were interested. To begin evaluating the success of each lead initiation type, a business analyst team would want to know the period of time for each initiation and subsequent response.

Lead Nurturing Metrics

Lead nurturing metrics focus on measuring leads as they move further along the pipeline of cold-to-warm lead interaction.

Lead Engagement Rate

Lead engagement rate measures exactly what it sounds like it measures. It measures the interaction points with prospects. From the interactions, a business can assess the best methods for progressing cold leads to becoming warm leads.

The internet has had a significant impact on the ways we engage with leads, so it is good to look at non-internet lead engagement and electronic lead engagement.

Non-Internet Lead Engagement

Does it matter how frequently a prospect is approached? Let's turn to our friends, the Girl Scouts, to demonstrate that concept. To give context, in the U.S., groups of girls form under an organization promoting the health, education, and empowerment of females under the age of 18. These girls are known for selling cookies to raise money for their activities.

One weekend afternoon, six Girl Scouts set up two tables with their cookies displayed, outside a supermarket. Three Girl Scouts go to one table, called Table J. Table J is outside Entry Point 1. Three Girl Scouts go to the other table, called Table K. Table K is outside Entry Point 2. On each table is the same number of cookie boxes of the same cookie type, displayed in the same arrangement. Assume one hundred people with equal quantities of money in their wallets go through Entry Point 1, and one hundred people with equal quantities of money in their wallets go through Entry Point 2.

For a period of three hours, the girls at Table J ask each individual entering the store to buy cookies. During the same three hours, the girls at Table K ask each individual entering the store and the same individuals exiting the store to buy cookies.

Table J sells 50 boxes of cookies, and Table K sells 75 boxes of cookies. It is a reasonable assumption that a second engagement with a prospect causes more individuals to buy cookies than if those same individuals were approached once.

Electronic Lead Engagement

Does it matter how frequently a prospect is approached? Let's stick with our Girl Scout friends. Instead of setting up tables of cookies outside a supermarket, let's say the same six Girl Scouts divide into two groups of three. Group J is a group of three, and Group K is a separate group of three.

Both groups, J and K, design an identical website. Each group emails their six grandparents to ask them to visit the website and order cookies. Assume that the grandparents for both groups are equally healthy, are similar from a socio-economic standpoint, and no grandparents have a power outage. Group K sends a second email to their set of six grandparents.

Group J sells 25 boxes of cookies, and Group K sells 23 boxes of cookies. It is a reasonable assumption that a second engagement with a prospect has less effect than one engagement when the engagement is done electronically.

Lead Conversion Metrics

Lead conversion metrics focus on measuring leads as they convert from prospects to leads. The most straightforward type of metric evaluates the number of leads that started as cold leads and converted to paying customers. Another way to evaluate lead conversion metrics is to consider what it costs the business to convert a lead to a customer. We will look at both.

Lead-to-Customer Conversion Rate

Lead-to-customer conversion rate is the number of leads who are identified and become customers. As with lead volume, a designated time period is needed in order to compare metrics.

Cost Per Lead-to-Customer Conversion

How much did it cost to take a potential lead from a cold lead, to evolving into a warm lead, to becoming a hot lead, and finally converting to becoming a customer? This metric is more complicated to determine. Parsing the cost of effort is challenging.

Basic math can show broad cost estimates for lead-to-customer conversions that involve only one type of interaction.

Assume a sales representative is compensated with an hourly wage as opposed to a yearly salary. The hourly wage is $25. If the sales representative spends three hours speaking and interacting directly with a prospect that converts to a customer (assuming the prospect has no other interaction with the business nor receives any other form of communication from the business), the cost of lead-to-customer conversion is $75.

What happens if a prospect is engaged at a conference, then comes to meet with the sales and product management teams, and also receives a follow-up email (that was one component of an outsourced public relations campaign)?

A few of the questions might be these. How much did it cost the business to attend the conference? That requires knowing travel fees, entrance fees, booth-constructing fees, etc. How much are the sales and product management teams' members paid, and what portion of their time was spent in the meeting? What was the cost of the public relations campaign, and what portion of the campaign was the issuance of the follow-up email?

As you can see, it is much more difficult to assign a cost to lead-to-customer conversion.

Revenue Metrics

Revenue metrics are used to measure the effectiveness of revenue optimization strategies. Two metrics that are helpful are revenue-per-lead and customer lifetime value.

Revenue-Per-Lead

Revenue per lead is a simple calculation. It's the total amount of new revenue brought in by leads divided by the number of sales-qualified leads (SQLs), usually over the span of the past quarter or the past year (Dillon, 2016).

That sounds easy enough to measure. It is, as long as everyone involved in revenue management as well as the sales and business analyst teams agree on definitions.

New revenue is revenue from a customer that didn't exist before a point in time. A sales-qualified lead is a prospect that has moved through the pipeline from being a cold lead to a hot lead.

Amazing Ampoules, a fictional business that manufactures single-use biodegradable pouches, sells a lot of its products to skincare companies. Since the trend of "green" beauty (i.e., Beauty products that do not create waste, have recyclable containers, or do not test on animals) is here to stay, many skincare companies are lining up for Amazing Ampoules' ampoules, which they will package serums, lotions, lip balms, etc.

Amazing Ampoules sells $1.5 million worth of ampoules to Fruity Facials. Fruity Facials has been a customer since 2020. Up until the last quarter of 2022, Fruity Facials has purchased $1.5 million in ampoules each year (2020 and 2021). In December of 2022, Fruity Facials ordered an additional $200,000 worth of ampoules. Amazing Ampoules can describe $200,000 of their total revenue from Fruity Facials as "new revenue."

Amazing Ampoules had two SQLs in 2022 that became customers by December 31, 2022:

- Beauty Company 01 with new revenue of $1 million

- Skin Iz Inn with new revenue of $500,000

For 2022, Amazing Ampoules had $1.7 million in new revenue. In total, they had three new leads.

$1,700,000 / 3 = $566,666 in revenue per lead

Though Amazing Ampoules is an existing customer, the $200,000 they added is new revenue. New revenue means that the amount is counted as a separate lead, though the customer has been a customer.

Customer Lifetime Value

Customer lifetime value (CLV) is a business metric that measures how much a business can plan to earn from the average customer over the course of the relationship (Caldwell, 2022).

CLV is more complex to calculate due to the variables involved. Also, it varies depending on the type of business (B2C or B2B) that is being evaluated, what they are selling (service or product or a combination of the two), and the duration for which they have a customer (e.g., grocery store customers may have different stores at which they purchase food, but it's unlikely that a hospital uses multiple medical records management software systems.)

In a B2C situation, a grocery store's customer can be expected to have an array of product purchases and frequent visits to procure the products. In a B2B situation, a customer buying magnetic resonance imaging equipment can be expected to buy much smaller quantities of the product and make less frequent purchases. Also, they are likely a business entity, not an individual.

B2C CLV

In the B2C situation, let's look at a grocery store and its customer, Angelo. To figure out what Angelo's CLV is, the grocery store looks at three variables. How many times in a week does Angelo shop at the grocery store? How much does Angelo spend, on average, for each visit? How many years is Angelo expected to be a customer?

Angelo shops twice per week. In one year, he is at the store 104 times (2 visits per week x 52 weeks = 104 visits). On average, he spends $50 per visit. In one year, he spends $5,200 ($50 per visit x 2 visits per week = $100 per week and $100 x 52 weeks = $5,200). Angelo has been shopping at the grocery store according to these patterns since he moved into the condominium complex next to the grocery store. He is friendly with the staff that bags his groceries and shared that he has two more years of medical school before he starts his residency. He doesn't know where that will be. The grocery store business analyst counts on Angelo's patronage for two years.

In order to calculate Angelo's future CLV, we look at his average number of visits per year, the quantity of money he spends per visit, and the anticipated number of years he will be a customer.

Angelo's CLV is 104 visits x $50 per visit x 2 years = $10,400.

B2B CLV

A software as a service company (SaaS) provides financial institutions with access to financial markets data. The investment professionals use the information from the data feed to advise their clients on their investment portfolios. Big Dollars Bank uses the SaaS services and pays $15,000 for a single data feed per month. Big Dollars Bank has been a SaaS customer for five years. They signed an addendum that commits them to another three years for the same data feed.

In order to calculate Big Dollars Bank's CLV, we look at the cost of the services for a period of time and the period of time they plan to use the services.

Big Dollars Bank's CLV is $15,000 per month x 96 months (60 months for the first five years and 36 months per the addendum) = $1,440,000.

A Final Word Regarding Metrics

This is the third time we have made the point that identifying and tracking metrics will not be consistent. Variables and their placement in a calculation will differ. Unlike the Pythagorean Theorem or the formula for a quadratic equation, which are fixed, the metrics used in revenue management vary. That does not mean that there are no definitive answers. It does mean that other considerations need to be made to ensure the calculations have value.

1. Data collection should be conducted over similar time periods (e.g., season, length of collection time).

2. More data points allow for a broader sample size. The broader the sample size, the more likely it is to replicate what happens in the population. We're sure you get this concept, but to add some humor, think of trying to find out what vegetables a three-year-old will eat. Imagine setting out broccoli, carrots, and red peppers. To establish what vegetable is most popular with three-year-olds, would you have three kids tested, or would you have three hundred kids tested? You likely would opt for three hundred. While there are far more three-year-olds in the world, three hundred is closer to the worldwide total than three is.

3. Metrics must be uniform for each evaluation. If you're tracking cold-to-warm leads in the first quarter of the year, in order to make an accurate comparison in the next year, you'll want to track cold-to-warm leads in the first quarter of the year.

Next up, we'll take some time with technology that is designed for measuring and optimizing metrics. It's the sequel to Chapter 3, where we glanced at the methods, analytics, and tracking available to assist us with understanding patterns and customer behavior.

Tools and Technologies for Measurement and Optimization

The topic might seem familiar to you since we covered a few mechanisms for tracking and measuring data in Chapter Three. We are going to hone our attention to the technology and tools used for measurement and optimization.

Marketing Automation Tools

As the name indicates, marketing automation tools are systems or software that allow marketing functions to be performed. The idea is that this will help streamline the marketing process, freeing professionals' time to pursue other marketing tasks that require hands-on interaction or a depth of assessment that a piece of technology can't touch.

Marketing automation tools are very similar (and some overlap) with marketing automation platforms. On the topic of marketing automation tools, we introduced functionalities like email automation, CRM updates, and lead scoring. Winnowing our way to the specifics of the tools themselves, we'll expand our view to include drip marketing, conditional workflows, and advanced techniques for rule-setting.

Drip Marketing

Drip marketing is a strategy that involves automatically sending out marketing emails on a schedule or based on user actions (Stych, 2022). It's a form of "intelligent" automated customer engagement. We say "intelligent" because the waterfall of actions is triggered by customer behaviors or the absence of customer behavior.

Examples of drip marketing include an automated response when a prospect signs up for an electronic newsletter, purchases some items in their electronic shopping cart but not all items, or registers for a live event. We can almost guarantee you have experienced drip marketing in the last 24 hours.

Customer Behavior Triggers

You enjoy 5K races that are held locally. You completed an electronic form for the Thanksgiving-themed race last fall. The same organization is hosting a spring-themed race in May. Through their drip marketing campaign that is electronically enabled, at a date specified by the organization, emails will be sent automatically to anyone who completed the electronic form for the Thanksgiving race.

Lack of Customer Behavior Triggers

You often shop online for books (you loved bookstores until people using their cell phones started browsing for books mid-conversation). You have purchased the first three mystery novels by P.D. James. You add the next two in the series, but you become distracted because your Saint Bernard ate a wood chip and is throwing up on your deck. You leave your computer to take care of him. By the time you have cleaned up your four-legged best friend, your two-legged children come home from school. There is football practice, then homework, and then dinner. Just before you turn in for the night, an email pops up, reminding you that you have P.D. James books that you're missing out on, as they are still in your online shopping cart.

Conditional Workflows

If you have ever taken a computer programming class, you might be familiar with "if…then…else" statements. They comprise the basics of computer programming. In its simplest form, an "if… then… else" statement is for the purpose of running a statement or a block of statements depending on the value of the condition (Microsoft Build, 2022). Said differently, "If the value of the condition is true, then call Function K, else call Function F."

Let's make this easier to understand. We'll set up a conditional workflow for booths at an amusement park. Ways 2 Amuze is an amusement park. To streamline admission to the park and to save money by not hiring people, Ways 2 Amuze installed automated booths at its entrance point, each with a locked gate. Each entrant must have a ticket to scan to be admitted. If they do not have a ticket, the gate will not allow them to pass through.

The condition is: The entrant has a ticket.

The value of the condition is true.

If the value is true, call Function K.

If the value is not true, call Function F.

Function K: Then gate opens

Function F: Else gate remains locked

If "the entrant has a ticket" (condition), the value of the condition is true, **then** Function K is called, **else** Function F is called.

Conditional workflows are a natural fit with the sales pipeline structure. Conditions can range from "called the prospect three times in three weeks" to "customer signs sales agreement." If…then…else statements can range from "if the condition is true, then send an email, else close CRM entry" to "if the condition is true, then make a telephone call, else, send a thank you email."

Data Analytics, Reporting, and Business Intelligence Technologies

Data analytics, reporting, and business intelligence are distinct from each other. That said, they overlap to a degree that it makes sense to cover the three functions together. One function often provides insight into another function, or looking at two of the functions together results in unique perspectives.

Data analytics and reporting functionalities broadly describe any method or technology that intakes data sets or raw information and transforms them/it through mathematical computations or logic-based rules to create an output identifying patterns (business intelligence). Businesses can study the patterns to recognize shifts, trends, and changes in their customers' behavior.

Business intelligence technologies allow users to work with reporting tools and data analytic outputs to accomplish these tasks.

- Pull data from multiple sources (e.g., spreadsheets and cloud storage) and integrate it into a comprehensive assessment. Said simply, if your employees have tracked gasket purchases (by type, material, stock-keeping unit number) in a spreadsheet and the consulting firm you hired processes client data through the cloud, a good BI tool can work the spreadsheet data into a format that can be "seen" by the cloud.

- Create visual representations that show user behavior over a period of time in context with user behavior over a different period of time. Dashboards, heat maps, graphics, charts, and cluster maps are types of visual representations.

- Utilize the data and raw information to build models and create predictive analytics. Predictive analytics are a computer's "best guesses" based on previous observations and quantitative findings.

- Share data and raw information as well as share analyses, summaries, flowcharts, etc., across departments and companies. This is an easy way to see how various departments are performing per their individual KPIs.

A Last Word

There is a lot to be learned and studied when it comes to the measurement and optimization of revenue management data. While we think every aspect of L2RM is important and valuable, we want to put an extra line under "measurement and optimization."

If something is unable to be measured, it cannot be optimized. If it cannot be optimized, it will remain stagnant. Something that is stagnant is not going to improve. If something is not improved, it is likely to become a second, third, or fourth choice…or not be an option at all. If your business is not an option to be chosen by a customer, it will lose revenue. Without revenue, it will not be profitable. If it is not profitable, it will fail.

Conclusion

L2RM has four characters. Who would have imagined that four characters could have so much potential and impact? Yet, here we are.

Our main goal is that businesses and the people comprising them realize that a solid L2RM process is money in the bank, not business baloney. *Profit Hacking: Unlocking Revenue, Maximizing Profit, Get the Lead and Keep the Lead! - Strategies for Explosive Profit Growth in the Modern Business World* had one job: ensure that readers across every industry and in every type of business understand that L2RM has processes, methods, and actions that result in practical strategies and greater revenue.

Let's take a look at the highlight reel.

Why L2RM Is a Necessity

How does a business earn revenue? It sells a product or a service for which there is a demand for a monetary amount that allows the business to pay its employees, pay its operating expenses, and earn a profit.

How do people become aware of a product or service? An ad interrupts their YouTube viewing. Their gym buddy mentions a wonderful new fitness coaching service. They receive a sample size of a face scrub in a "free gift" box from a skincare company.

How do you draw these people to *your* business's product or service? Take note of the first link in the L2RM chain: lead generation.

Why L2RM Is Relevant

L2RM is the set of processes, methods, and actions that take a cold lead to revenue. Many businesses have cold leads; someone only needs to have a conversation, send an email, or launch an advertising campaign to initiate lead generation. (Please understand, we are not trivializing the process of lead generation; we are noting what starts it, not the process itself.)

Between getting the word out about your product or service and earning revenue from paying customers lies a series of links that comprise the L2RM chain.

These links include:

1. Lead generation

2. Lead nurturing

3. Lead conversion

4. Lead management

5. Lead measurement and optimization

6. Revenue management

Links In a Chain

We spent a lot of time and energy focusing on the links existing and working in context with one another. One of the many unique facets of L2RM is that each link in the chain (listed above) is composed of discrete actions, and at the same time, each link in the chain comprises the chain as a whole.

For a visualization exercise, imagine the plastic interconnecting blocks you may have played with as a child. Let's say you made a fence from the plastic interconnecting blocks. One fence post was made up of six blocks, and twelve fence posts created a fence. The individual blocks were made up of posts, and the posts made up the whole fence.

Again, refer to the list above and see that lead nurturing is point number two in the chain of L2RM. Lead nurturing involves personalization, a call to action, lead scoring, lead magnets, and retargeting; these are links that make up the lead nurturing link that is a link in the L2RM chain.

Metrics, Measurement, and Optimization

Lead generation, lead nurturing, lead conversion, lead management, and revenue management are often expensive and time-intensive exercises. Hundreds, if not thousands, of hours are spent on these business processes. They involve the skills, abilities, and talents of a cast of thousands. Everyone from the new guy making cold calls up through the chief revenue officer in the C-suite is involved.

Where Is the Proof?

Supervisor: "What's the value?"

Employee: "Oh, well, L2RM activities cost a lot, and we have some very sharp people tasked with these activities! Look at this 40-slide deck of graphs, charts, and heat maps!"

Supervisor: "What's the value?"

Employee: "As I said, L2RM activities cost a lot. We hired some subject matter experts that have a combined fifty years of experience. Also, the business analysts that worked on the L2RM activities have data science degrees from-"

Supervisor: "You're telling me about your L2RM programs. You're describing the employees involved as well as expounding on their work histories. For some odd reason, you're also reading redacted versions of their resumes. I want to see proof that the L2RM processes have value."

Employee: (...)

Are you perspiring yet? We are, and we wrote the text. All joking aside, the supervisor's question remained unanswered.

The employee that provided responses, which unfortunately didn't answer the question, described the L2RM activities and talked about the aspects that are positive. The responses did not show empirical evidence or quantitative results demonstrating L2RM's benefits.

Here's the Proof!

Supervisor: "What's the value?"

Employee: "L2RM activities cost 15% of the annual budget. Our top competitor, based on market share, spends about 25% of their annual budget on L2RM activities. We should invest more in L2RM activities."

Supervisor: "How do you know about our top competitor's budget?"

Employee: "The competitor was interviewed in industry journals, and they answered questions about the importance of L2RM technology. In one interview, a representative gave approximations of how much their new L2RM system cost. I checked out the system. It cost "X" dollars based on the most common configuration. For the system alone, "X" dollars is 20% of our budget."

Supervisor: "So you want to increase our budget because of some verbal faux pas during an interview?"

Employee: "Also, the three business analysts we recently hired completed a case study for their senior project. It showed evidence that spending money on L2RM activities was anticipated to increase by 37% in the next calendar year."

Supervisor: "You're telling me that we should base our spending on the findings of a class project?"

Employee: "The case study was published in *The Most Prestigious Financial Magazine That Ever Existed In All the Universe.*"

Supervisor: "Okay, I'm listening."

Employee: "I am suggesting that our top competitor's interviewee information, my research into the system they use, and the evidence in the business analysts' senior project give three compelling reasons to increase our L2RM expenditure."

Supervisor: "Get me some more insights into the L2RM activities across our industry. Then we will talk."

In this conversation, the employee provided responses that included verifiable data (i.e., the supervisor could read the same article in the industry journal), research, and cited the acceptance of a recognized third party (the fictional publication titled *The Most Prestigious Financial Magazine That Ever Existed In All the Universe*). The responses showed empirical evidence and quantitative data points supporting the idea that the L2RM budget should be increased.

Peter's Proof

Do you recall Prokofiev's musical tale of a child named Peter who made up harrowing stories about a hungry wolf? Many times, Peter yelled for help, even though there was no wolf near him. Each time, people responded to his cries and tales of woe. They never saw a wolf because there wasn't one. One day, there was a wolf. Unfortunately, it was hungry, and it ate Peter.

Let's add to the story and state that nothing was left of poor Peter. Remember, the wolf was really hungry. The people didn't believe there was a wolf since there was never one in previous instances. Perhaps they thought Peter ran away or went on a (very long) camping trip.

Now, had this story taken place in modern times, Peter would have posted pictures to his social media account that showed the wolf approaching. Assuming there was a Wi-Fi signal and also assuming that the wolf didn't scarf Peter's phone before the pictures were uploaded, there would be proof that Peter was eaten by a wolf.

What was the proof? The proof was the photos on Peter's social media. The proof was irrefutable.

Metrics and Measurement

There are L2RM methods that allow the creation of tangible results. These tangible results are determined to be successful or not successful based on metrics. *The metrics used to evaluate L2RM processes are able to show quantitative fluctuations by using empirical inputs and measurable outputs.*

That first paragraph may sound like we are entering into the "business blather" department again, but let's break apart the sentence to see that it makes total sense.

"The metrics used to evaluate L2RM processes,"

This portion of the sentence refers to the standards and benchmarks we use to determine the value of the L2RM processes a business uses.

Metrics used to evaluate L2RM include:

- lead volume

- lead-to-customer conversion rate

- lead-to-sales conversion rate

- lead engagement rate

- revenue per lead

- customer lifetime value

How do you know if July or October was a better month for prospect interaction? You can look at the lead engagement rate for each July and October. If someone asks you, "Which month was better?" you might say, "It depends on what variables you're considering. I can tell you the lead engagement rate for July and for October. We can assess those two months regarding lead engagement."

"... are able to show quantitative fluctuations,"

This portion of the sentence declares that metrics are able to demonstrate the movement of the metrics. Quantitative fluctuations might indicate how many more leads were identified in the third quarter versus the fourth quarter of the same year or how many leads were converted to sales in January versus December of the same year.

"The weather next week looks much better for a picnic than this week's weather."

The aforesaid is an example of a qualitative fluctuation. There is no forecast of the weather for this week, nor is there a forecast of the weather for next week. There is no variable to measure (i.e., are we talking about temperature, precipitation, or the UV index?). As such, the statement about the weather is not objective and cannot be proven.

That the fluctuations are quantitative simply means the direction a metric is moving is able to be measured objectively.

16 Hot Leads

"There were 16 hot leads identified in the second quarter that went through an A/B test. Of the 16, 11 leads reported a preference for option M and 5 leads reported a preference for option N."

The aforestated is an example of a quantitative fluctuation. The number of hot leads was counted; there were 16, and they went through an A/B test. There were 11 hot leads that preferred option M and there were 5 hot leads that preferred option N. If you are asked which option was more popular, you can say, "Option M was more popular." If you are challenged, you can say, "Eleven hot leads chose option M of the sixteen hot leads that went through the A/B test. Five hot leads chose option N. Eleven hot leads is six more than five hot leads."

"… by using empirical inputs and measurable outputs."

This portion of the sentence explains how the metrics used can show quantitative fluctuations. "Empirical inputs and measurable outputs" means that the variables used in the L2RM processes are observable without subjectivity, and the outputs are able to be counted and compared through the act of measuring.

Empirical inputs include numbers, percentages, and ranges. Examples include the number of customers, the percentage of users, and the age ranges of prospects. One can count customers. One can count the portion of users compared to the population of users. One can count the spread of prospects' ages. "Measurable outputs" simply mean that the results (the outputs) can be quantified.

Are Qualitative Statements Relevant?

"We have happy customers" is a qualitative statement. The customers are demonstrating behaviors and feelings belying a recognizably jubilant mindset. We cannot prove if they are happy by counting them or counting some aspect of the customers.

That isn't to say that qualitative results are less important than quantifiable results.

"We have happy customers" is something any business would be delighted to tout. When a business has to make choices about where their time, effort, and money will be spent, they'll want those resources directed towards products and services that make the customers happy.

It is so critical to be able to know what makes the customers happy, and the only way to do this is through metrics and measuring. A business can focus on having happy customers by using metrics and measurement.

Metrics indicative of happy customers might include:

1. A set of existing customers return to buy another product or sign up for another time period of service.

2. The number of products or services consumed by existing customers increases from one quarter to another.

3. There was an increase of 67 new customer referrals from existing customers during the second quarter of 2022 to the third quarter of 2022. For the first quarter to the second quarter of 2022, there were no new customer referrals from existing customers.

4. Of a zero to five-star rating system, in February of 2021, the average rating was three stars, based on one set of 100 customers that visited the restaurant on weekend days between 5 p.m. and 7 p.m.

Of a zero to five-star rating system with the same variables included in the rating system, in March of 2021, the average rating was four stars, based on another set of 100 customers that visited the restaurant on weekend days between 5 p.m. and 7 p.m. The customer reviews from March are more favorable.

Optimization

Optimization of L2RM processes can be initiated once the metrics are measured. Remember, once a thing (concrete or abstract) can be measured, it can be improved in a tangible and trackable way.

Optimization of the 16 Hot Leads

Refer to the 16 hot leads example. Recall that "There were 16 hot leads identified in the second quarter that went through an A/B test. Of the 16, 11 hot leads reported a preference for option M and 5 leads reported a preference for option N."

If you're concerned about converting these hot leads to customers, what might you ask the teams of product development and product management to focus on? Let's see. The preference for option M was demonstrated by 11 hot leads. The preference for option N was demonstrated by 5 hot leads. More than double the number of hot leads liked option M better than option N. You are going to tell your product development and product management teams to spend time, effort, and money on option N.

In a perfect world full of all the time, energy, and financial resources one could want, it would be great to evaluate option N, too. After all, five hot leads preferred option N. However, it isn't a perfect world. Businesses do not have surpluses of time, energy, or financial resources. Thus, they must devote what they do have to the products and services that are preferred. In our example, that product is option M.

The Final Word

You know the links in the L2RM chain, and you know the pieces that built the links. You know the front office manager, the person who waters the plants, the data-loving analyst, the sales representative, and you (regardless of your role) are part of the lead nurturing phase.

You can teach a short course on lead conversion step-by-step. Then you can list the functions that a good marketing automation platform performs. If anyone asks, you'll be able to lay out an if…then…else statement to solve a problem. Should your child or nephew argue that the branded chocolate chip cookies are much better than the off-brand chocolate chip cookies, you can direct them to set up an A/B test, which may not convince them, but it will keep them occupied for a couple of hours.

While we're at the end of our book, you're just getting started.

Afterword

Your input and feedback through reviews are tremendously important. They guide others in their decision to explore this book. If you've found fresh insights, been led to reconsider your perspectives, discovered practical actions for change, or affirmed your current effective practices, we invite you to share your experiences in a review. Your endorsement would mean the world to us, so if you can spare 5 minutes, I would truly appreciate it. I can't thank you enough for your support and your role in this book's success - you make a big difference!

If you found value in this book and want to further your learning journey, I regularly share thoughts on leadership, mindset, and business on my blog. You're more than welcome to subscribe and join our community: https://magneticmindsetblog.com/

Finally, I am grateful for your commitment, both in reading this book and sharing your thoughts. Your involvement is priceless in ensuring the sustained growth of the Magnetic Mindset Leadership. We're excited to hear from you!

With gratitude,

Thomas Allan

References

Alderton, M. (2022, November 10). *Vicarious surgical robotic system: The 200 best inventions of 2022*. Time. https://time.com/collection/best-inventions-2022/6230032/vicarious-surgical-robotic-system/

Aston, B. (2023, April 21). *10 best user behavior analytics tools to assess product use in 2022*. The Product Manager. https://theproductmanager.com/tools/best-user-behavior-analytics-tools/

Bailey, M. (2022, September 29). *What is the Mendoza Line in baseball? Mario Mendoza stat explained*. Baseball Bible.net. https://www.baseballbible.net/what-is-the-mendoza-line/

Balz, M., Burke, A., Montagner, A., & Tarallo, M. (2021, December 21). *A new operating model for pharma: How the pandemic has influenced priorities* | McKinsey. https://www.mckinsey.com/industries/life-sciences/our-insights/a-new-operating-model-for-pharma-how-the-pandemic-has-influenced-priorities

Birkett, A. (2022, September 9). *The 14 best marketing automation software tools available to you*. https://blog.hubspot.com/marketing/marketing-automation-software-tools

Caldwell, A. (2021, April 13). *How to calculate customer lifetime value.*
Oracle NetSuite.
https://www.netsuite.com/portal/resource/articles/ecommerce/custo
mer-lifetime-value-clv.shtml

Carmicheal, K. (2020, March 24). *Why website indexation is a must-have
for marketers.* https://blog.hubspot.com/marketing/website-indexation

Chomsky, N., & Mcchesney, R. W. (2011). *Profit over people : neoliberalism
and the global order.* Seven Stories Press.

CMI. (2021). *What is content marketing?* Content Marketing Institute.
https://contentmarketinginstitute.com/what-is-content-marketing/

Cohen, O., Fox, B., Mills, N., & Wright, P. (n.d.). *Coronavirus in pharma
commercial: an uneven recovery |* McKinsey.
https://www.mckinsey.com/industries/life-sciences/our-insights/covid-
19-and-commercial-pharma-navigating-an-uneven-recovery

Dcruz, N. (2021, October 26). *Functions of operations management: know
about its importance.*
https://www.mygreatlearning.com/blog/functions-of-operations-mana
gement-know-about-its-importance/#:~:text=Planning%2C%20organizi
ng%2C%20and%20strategizing%20the

Decker, A. (2021, May 30). *The ultimate guide to sales strategy.*
https://blog.hubspot.com/sales/sales-strategy

Dillon, C. (2016, July 7). *The metric that helps maximize sales efficiency.*
Mattermark.
https://mattermark.com/how-to-calculate-revenue-per-lead/

Duggal, N. (2021, June 1). T*op 7 types of leads in business [plus ways to
convert them].*
https://www.simplilearn.com/types-of-leads-in-business-article

Ellis, L., & Anderson, M. (2012). *The dash.* Thomas Nelson Inc.

Erin Gilliam Haije. (2018, July 19). *Top 15 business intelligence tools: an overview*. Mopinion.
https://mopinion.com/business-intelligence-bi-tools-overview/

Fernando, J. (2022, August 23). *Margin and margin trading explained plus advantages and disadvantages*. Investopedia.
https://www.investopedia.com/terms/m/margin.asp#:~:text=What%20
Does%20It%20Mean%20to

Fitzgerald, A. (2022, September 21). *A beginner's guide to web analytics*.
https://blog.hubspot.com/marketing/guide-to-web-analytics-traffic-ter
ms

Fragapane, R. (2021, June 15). *How heat maps are used for business mapping*. Maptive.
https://www.maptive.com/heat-maps-for-business/

Gallo, A. (2017, June 28). *A refresher on A/B testing*. Harvard Business Review.
https://hbr.org/2017/06/a-refresher-on-ab-testing

Gervais, R., Daniels, G., & Merchant, S. (2005, March 24). *The office* [Television series].

Grigoryev, M. (2022, July 19). *Cold, warm & hot leads: what is the difference for b2b sales*. GetProspect.
https://getprospect.com/blog/difference-between-cold-warm-hot-lead
s

Guay, M. (2022, September 19). *Zapier paths: A smarter way to build conditional workflows*.
https://zapier.com/blog/zapier-paths-conditional-workflows/

Hillier, W. (2023, April 5). *The 9 best data analytics tools [For 2021 and beyond]*.
https://careerfoundry.com/en/blog/data-analytics/data-analytics-tools
/

Homer. (2018). *The odyssey* (E. Wilson, Trans.). W.W. Norton and Company.

if then else statement | Encyclopedia.com. (n.d.). Www.encyclopedia.com. Retrieved May 9, 2023, from https://www.encyclopedia.com/computing/dictionaries-thesauruses-pictures-and-press-releases/if-then-else-statement

Indeed, E. T. (2022, September 30). *What is revenue management?* (definition and strategies). Indeed Career Guide. https://www.indeed.com/career-advice/career-development/what-is-revenue-management

Karabay, G. (2022, August 2). *7 winning lead generation examples for 2022*. Outfunnel - Sales & Marketing Workflow Platform. https://outfunnel.com/lead-generation-examples/

Kelwig, D. (2023, January 4). *The ultimate lead nurturing guide for 2023 (strategy & statistics)*. Zendesk. https://www.zendesk.com/blog/ultimate-guide-lead-nurturing/

Kimball, D. (2012, July 26). *Case study: cards against humanity*. Kickstarter. https://www.kickstarter.com/blog/case-study-cards-against-humanity

Kolowich, L. (2021, August 17). *Lead generation: a beginner's guide to generating business leads the inbound way*. https://blog.hubspot.com/marketing/beginner-inbound-lead-generation-guide-ht

Kolowich, L. (2022, August 23). *Lead scoring 101: how to use data to calculate a basic lead score*. https://blog.hubspot.com/marketing/lead-scoring-instructions

Kumar Srivastav, A. (2021, January 9). *Revenue management*. WallStreetMojo. https://www.wallstreetmojo.com/revenue-management/

Kumar, A. (2022, September 12). *What are the roles and responsibilities of an operations manager* | Emeritus India. Emeritus - Online Certificate Courses | Diploma Programs. https://emeritus.org/in/learn/roles-and-responsibilities-of-an-operations-manager/

Laurel, C. T. U. 11301 S. R., & Md 20708 800.950.1992. (2023, April 13). *Walmart sets the standard with supply chain automation.* https://www.captechu.edu/blog/walmart-sets-standard-supply-chain-automation

Lucas, G. (Director). (1999, May 19). *The phantom menace* [Film]. 20th Century Fox.

Marr, B. (2022, December 6). *The top 5 healthcare trends in 2023.* Forbes. https://www.forbes.com/sites/bernardmarr/2022/12/06/the-top-5-healthcare-trends-in-2023/?sh=240018f7565b

Michaels, J. (2020, June 18). *10 free food subscription boxes to try for free meals & snacks.* Frugal for Less. https://www.frugalforless.com/food-subscription-boxes/

Nachlas, C. (2015, December 8). *Why we eat fruitcake on christmas.* The Daily Meal. https://www.thedailymeal.com/holidays/why-we-eat-fruitcake-christmas

Ninjas, N. (2023, February 23). *Newbook - what is a revenue management system (RMS)?* NewBook. https://www.newbook.cloud/what-is-a-revenue-management-system-rms/

o365devx. (2022, January 22). *Using If...Then...Else statements (VBA).* https://learn.microsoft.com/en-us/office/vba/language/concepts/getting-started/using-ifthenelse-statements

Patchett, A. (2004). *The magician's assistant.* HarperCollins.

Patel, S. (2021, January 20). *12 Important lead generation metrics & KPIs to track in 2021*. REVE Chat.
https://www.revechat.com/blog/lead-generation-kpis/

Pricing analysts: what they do & why they're so important for business. (n.d.).
https://www.paddle.com/resources/pricing-analysts

Rao, A. R., Bergen, M. E., & Davis, S. (2000, March). *How to fight a price war*. Harvard Business Review.
https://hbr.org/2000/03/how-to-fight-a-price-war

Rinko, S. (2022, January 28). *Inbound vs outbound lead generation: meanings & which to do*.
https://sellingsignals.com/inbound-vs-outbound-lead-generation/

Sergey Prokofiev, Williams, M., & Sergei Prokofiev. (2018). *Peter and the wolf*. Pearson Education.

7Learnings. (2021, March 15). *Price optimization: what is it? How is it done today*? 7Learnings.
https://7learnings.com/blog/what-is-price-optimization/

Severn, W. (2023, April 21). P*roduct availability - 6 tips on how to improve it*.
https://www.slimstock.com/blog/product-availability/

Snyder Bulik, B. (2020, March 17). *Grounded by the pandemic, pharma reps turn to digital tools to reach docs*. FiercePharma.
https://www.fiercepharma.com/marketing/pharma-sales-reps-stay-home-minimize-face-time-physicians-as-covid-19-spread-continues

Strauss, L. (2023, March 15). *What is lead management and how do you do it right*? | Zapier.
https://zapier.com/blog/lead-management/

Stych, J. (2022, September 16). *Drip marketing: what is it and how is it done?* | Zapier. https://zapier.com/blog/drip-marketing/

Tempkin, M., Dillon, J., Halpern, E., Hantoot, B., Munk, D., Pinsof, D., & Weinstein, E. (2010). *Cards Against Humanity* [Cards].

The ultimate guide to marketing automation | Online Digital Marketing Courses. (2022, December 22). https://digitalmarketinginstitute.com/blog/the-ultimate-guide-to-marketing-automation

Twin, A. (2023, March 22). *Understanding key performance indicators (KPI)*. Investopedia. https://www.investopedia.com/terms/k/kpi.asp

Vallender, P. (2019, May 12). *Inbound vs. outbound lead generation, the differences and similarities.* https://www.blendb2b.com/blog/inbound-vs-outbound-lead-generation-differences-and-similarities

Van Arnum, P. (2020, August 5). *Profits and pharma: the impact of COVID-19. DCAT value chain insights.* https://www.dcatvci.org/features/profits-and-pharma-the-impact-of-covid-19/

Watch, M. (n.d.). *How to calculate engagement rate: 12 KPIs to track.* Metrics Watch. https://metricswatch.com/how-to-calculate-engagement-rate

Weisman, A. (2014, May 19). *"Silicon Valley" had to make an insane number of burger king runs to shoot this brilliant scene.* Business Insider. https://www.businessinsider.com/silicon-valley-set-designer-explains-hamburger-scene-2014-5

What is outbound lead generation? 7 strategies for successful sales. (n.d.). Www.cognism.com. Retrieved April 22, 2023, from:

https://www.cognism.com/outbound-lead-generation#:~:text=What%2
0are%20outbound%20leads%3F

What is social media monitoring? (2019). BigCommerce.
https://www.bigcommerce.com/ecommerce-answers/what-social-med
ia-monitoring/

Which types of steel beams should you order? (2022, October 3). Intsel
Steel/Bushwick Metals.
https://www.bushwickmetals.com/types-of-steel-beams-order/#:~:text
=Most%20commonly%2C%20steel%20beams%20come

www.ingramcontent.com/pod-product-compliance
Lightning Source LLC
Chambersburg PA
CBHW060043030426
42334CB00019B/2470